WORLD OF ANIMALS

44

AMPHIBIANS AND REPTILES

LIZARDS 1

Agamas, Chameleons, Iguanas ...

CHRIS MATTISON, VALERIE DAVIES

GROLIER

an imprint of

SCHOLASTIC

www.scholastic.com/librarypublishing

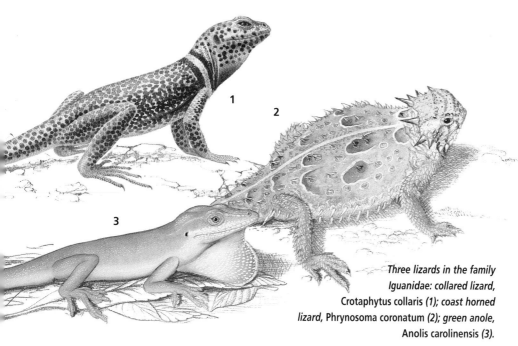

Three lizards in the family Iguanidae: collared lizard, Crotaphytus collaris (1); coast horned lizard, Phrynosoma coronatum (2); green anole, Anolis carolinensis (3).

Published 2005 by Grolier, an imprint of Scholastic Library Publishing
Danbury, CT 06816

This edition published exclusively for the school and library market

The Brown Reference Group plc.
(incorporating Andromeda Oxford Limited)
8 Chapel Place
Rivington Street
London
EC2A 3DQ

© 2005 The Brown Reference Group plc.

Library of Congress Cataloging-in-Publication Data

Amphibians and Reptiles.
    p. cm. -- (World of Animals; v. 41-50)
    Contents: [1] Salamanders, newts, and caecilians / Chris Mattison -- [2] Frogs and toads 1 / Chris Mattison -- [3] Frogs and toads 2 / Chris Mattison -- [4] Lizards 1 / Valerie Davies, Chris Mattison -- [5] Lizards 2 / Chris Mattison -- [6] Lizards 3 / Valerie Davies, Chris Mattison -- [7] Turtles and crocodilians / David Alderton -- [8] Snakes 1 / Chris Mattison -- [9] Snakes 2 / Chris Mattison -- [10] Snakes 3 / Chris Mattison.
    ISBN 0-7172-5916-1 (set : alk. paper) -- ISBN 0-7172-5917-X (v. 1 : alk. paper) -- ISBN 0-7172-5918-8 (v. 2 : alk. paper) -- ISBN 0-7172-5919-6 (v. 3 : alk. paper) -- ISBN 0-7172-5920-X (v. 4 : alk. paper) -- ISBN 0-7172-5921-8 (v. 5 : alk. paper) -- ISBN 0-7172-5922-6 (v. 6 : alk. paper) -- ISBN 0-7172-5923-4 (v. 7 : alk. paper) -- ISBN 0-7172-5924-2 (v. 8 : alk. paper) -- ISBN 0-7172-5925-0 (v. 9 : alk. paper) -- ISBN 0-7172-5926-9 (v. 10 : alk. paper)
    1. Amphibians -- Juvenile literature. 2. Reptiles -- Juvenile literature [1. Amphibians. 2. Reptiles.] I. Grolier (Firm) II. Series: World of Animals (Danbury, Conn.); v. 41-50.
QL49.W877 2003
590--dc22   2002073860

Set ISBN 0-7172-5916-1

Project Directors: Graham Bateman, Lindsey Lowe
Editors: Virginia Carter, Angela Davies
Art Editor and Designer: Steve McCurdy
Picture Manager: Becky Cox
Picture Researcher: Alison Floyd
Main Artists: Denys Ovenden, Philip Hood, Myke Taylor, Ken Oliver, Michael Woods, David M. Dennis
Maps: Steve McCurdy, Tim Williams
Production: Alastair Gourlay, Maggie Copeland

Printed in Singapore

About This Volume

This is the first volume in the *World of Animals* series to deal with reptiles. It begins with general information that applies to the 8,000 or so species of reptiles as a whole, followed by an introduction to the lizard group. The volume then describes, with examples, four groups of lizards—tuataras, agamas, chameleons, and iguanas.

Although they look like lizards, the tuataras are unique and ancient reptiles that have more in common with species that lived many millions of years ago than with other modern reptiles. They survive today only on a handful of small islands off New Zealand.

The lizards are the most conspicuous reptiles and are especially numerous in warm climates. They adapt well to a variety of environmental conditions and are present in most places from rain forests to deserts. There are several aquatic and semiaquatic species. One, the Galápagos marine iguana, regularly enters the sea to feed. The agamas, chameleons, and iguanas are all covered in this volume. Agamas and iguanas include many large, showy species in which males in particular are extremely colorful. They often develop horns, crests, dewlaps, and other ornamentation for use in territorial or courtship displays. Chameleons are famous for their ability to change color—a talent that is often exaggerated—but these fascinating reptiles have several other unique characteristics, such as their ability to catch insects with the sticky end of a long, protrusible tongue, and independently swiveling eye turrets.

Contents

The frilled lizard, Chlamydosaurus kingii from Australia, adopts a unique and impressive defensive display.

The large horns on male Jackson's chameleons, Chamaeleo jacksonii, are used for fighting and defense.

The spiny tailed dab lizard, Uromastyx acanthinurus, protects itself from predators with its well-armored tail.

How to Use This Set

World of Animals: Amphibians and Reptiles is a 10-volume set that describes in detail reptiles and amphibians from all corners of the earth. Each volume brings together those animals that are most closely related and have similar lifestyles. So all the frogs and toads are in Volumes 42 and 43, the snakes are in Volumes 48, 49, and 50, and so on. To help you find volumes that interest you, look at pages 6 and 7 (Find the Animal). A brief introduction to each volume is also given on page 2 (About This Volume).

Article Styles

Each volume contains two types of article. The first kind introduces major groups (such as amphibians, reptiles, frogs and toads, or lizards). It presents a general overview of the subject.

The second type of article makes up most of each volume. It describes in detail individual species, such as the American bullfrog or the American alligator, or groups of very similar animals, such as reed frogs or day geckos. Each article starts with a fact-filled **data panel** to help you gather information at a glance. Used together, the two different styles of article will enable you to become familiar with animals in the context of their evolutionary history and biological relationships.

Data panel presents basic statistics of each animal

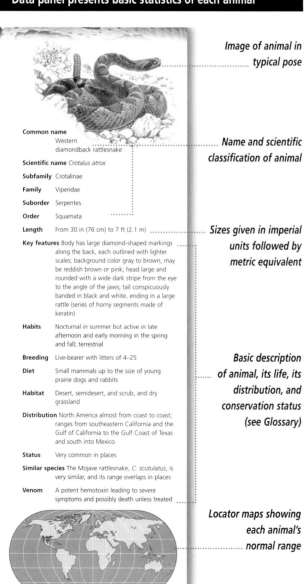

Image of animal in typical pose

Name and scientific classification of animal

Common name Western diamondback rattlesnake

Scientific name *Crotalus atrox*

Subfamily Crotalinae

Family Viperidae

Suborder Serpentes

Order Squamata

Length From 30 in (76 cm) to 7 ft (2.1 m)

Key features Body has large diamond-shaped markings along the back, each outlined with lighter scales; background color gray to brown, may be reddish brown or pink; head large and rounded with a wide dark stripe from the eye to the angle of the jaws; tail conspicuously banded in black and white, ending in a large rattle (series of horny segments made of keratin)

Habits Nocturnal in summer but active in late afternoon and early morning in the spring and fall; terrestrial

Breeding Live-bearer with litters of 4–25

Diet Small mammals up to the size of young prairie dogs and rabbits

Habitat Desert, semidesert, arid scrub, and dry grassland

Distribution North America almost from coast to coast; ranges from southeastern California and the Gulf of California to the Gulf Coast of Texas and south into Mexico

Status Very common in places

Similar species The Mojave rattlesnake, *C. scutulatus*, is very similar, and its range overlaps in places

Venom A potent hemotoxin leading to severe symptoms and possibly death unless treated

Sizes given in imperial units followed by metric equivalent

Basic description of animal, its life, its distribution, and conservation status (see Glossary)

Locator maps showing each animal's normal range

Article describes a particular animal

Scientific name of animal

Common name of animal

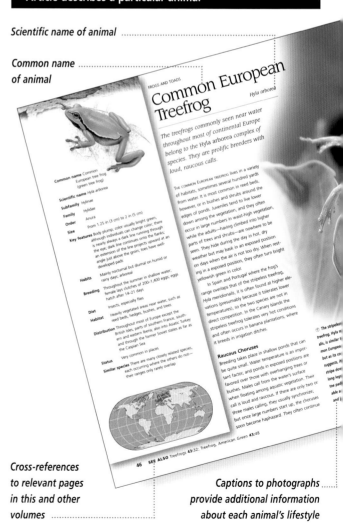

FROGS AND TOADS

Common European Treefrog

Hyla arborea

The treefrogs commonly seen near water throughout most of continental Europe belong to the Hyla arborea complex of species. They are prolific breeders with loud, raucous calls.

THE COMMON EUROPEAN TREEFROG lives in a variety of habitats, sometimes several hundred yards from water. It is most common in reed beds, however, or in bushes and shrubs around the edges of ponds. Juveniles tend to live lower down among the vegetation, and they often occur in large numbers in waist-high vegetation, while the adults—having climbed into higher parts of trees and shrubs—are nowhere to be seen. They hide during the day in hot, dry weather but may bask in an exposed position on days when the air is not too dry. When resting in an exposed position, they often turn bright yellowish green in color.

In Spain and Portugal where the frog's range overlaps that of the stripeless treefrog, *Hyla meridionalis*, it is often found at higher elevations (presumably because it tolerates lower temperatures), so the two species are not in direct competition. In the Canary Islands the stripeless treefrog tolerates very hot conditions and often occurs in banana plantations, where it breeds in irrigation ditches.

Common name Common European tree frog (green tree frog)

Scientific name Hyla arborea

Subfamily Hylinae

Family Hylidae

Order Anura

Size From 1.25 in (3 cm) to 2 in (5 cm)

Key features Body plump, color usually bright green, although individuals can change color; there is nearly always a dark line running through the eye; dark line continues onto the flanks; an extension of the line projects upward at an angle just above the groin; toes have well-developed pads

Habits Mainly nocturnal but diurnal on humid or rainy days; arboreal

Breeding Throughout the summer in shallow water; female lays clutches of 200–1,400 eggs; eggs hatch after 14–21 days

Diet Insects, especially flies

Habitat Heavily vegetated areas near water, such as reed beds, hedges, bushes, and trees

Distribution Throughout most of Europe except the British Isles, parts of southern France, southern and eastern Iberia, also into Asiatic Turkey and through the former Soviet states as far as the Caspian Sea

Status Very common in places

Similar species There are many closely related species, each occurring where the others do not—their ranges only rarely overlap

Raucous Choruses

Breeding takes place in shallow ponds that can be quite small. Water temperature is an important factor, and ponds in exposed positions are favored over those with overhanging trees or bushes. Males call from the water's surface when floating among aquatic vegetation. Their call is loud and raucous. If there are only two or three males calling, they usually synchronize, but once large numbers start up, the choruses soon become haphazard. They continue

The stripeless treefrog, Hyla meridionalis, is similar to the common European... but as its name suggests, stripe down... long tail... toe pad... able to... and t...

46 SEE ALSO Treefrogs 43:32; Treefrog, American Green 43:48

Cross-references to relevant pages in this and other volumes

Captions to photographs provide additional information about each animal's lifestyle

A number of other features help you navigate through the volumes and present you with helpful extra information. At the bottom of many pages are **cross-references** to other articles of interest. They may be to related animals, animals that live in similar places, or that have similar behavior, predators (or prey), lifestyles, and much more. Each volume also contains a **Set Index** to the complete *World of Animals: Amphibians and Reptiles*. Animals mentioned in the text are indexed by common and scientific names, and many topics are also covered. There is also a **Glossary** that will help you understand certain technical words. Each volume includes lists of useful **Further Reading and Websites** that help you take your research further.

Graphic full-color photographs bring text to life

Easy-to-read and comprehensive text

Tables summarize classification of groups

Detailed diagrams illustrate text

Who's Who tables summarize classification of each major group

At-a-glance boxes cover topics of special interest

Meticulous drawings illustrate a typical selection of group members

Introductory article describes family or closely related groups

Introductory article describes major groups of animals

5

Find the Animal

World of Animals: Amphibians and Reptiles is the fifth part of a library that describes all groups of living animals. Each cluster of volumes in *World of Animals* covers a familiar group of animals—mammals, birds, reptiles and amphibians, fish, and insects and other invertebrates.

The Animal Kingdom

The living world is divided into five kingdoms, one of which (kingdom Animalia) is the main subject of the *World of Animals*. Kingdom Animalia is divided into major groups called phyla. The phylum Chordata contains those animals that have a backbone—mammals, birds, reptiles, amphibians, and fish. Animals without backbones (so-called invertebrates, such as insects, spiders, mollusks, and crustaceans) belong to many different phyla. To find which set of volumes in the *World of Animals* you need, see the chart below.

World of Animals: Amphibians and Reptiles deals with two of the oldest lineages of land animals—the amphibians, which evolved from fish some 400 million years ago, and the reptiles, which evolved from amphibians about 350 million years ago. Although they are no longer dominant animals on earth (unlike the early reptiles typified by the dinosaurs), over 5,000 amphibian species and 8,000 species of reptiles can still be found. Most live in warmer or tropical regions of the world.

Naming Animals

To discuss animals, names are needed for the different kinds. Western diamondback rattlesnakes are one kind of snake, and sidewinders are another.

Rank	Scientific name	Common name
Kingdom	Animalia	Animals
Phylum	Chordata	Animals with a backbone
Class	Reptilia	Reptiles
Order	Squamata	Lizards, Snakes, Amphisbaenians
Suborder	Serpentes	Snakes
Family	Viperidae	Vipers and Pit Vipers
Genus	*Crotalus*	Rattlesnakes
Species	*Crotalus atrox*	Western diamondback rattlesnake

The kingdom Animalia is subdivided into phyla, classes, orders, families, genera, and species. Above is the classification for the western diamondback rattlesnake.

All western diamondback rattlesnakes look alike, breed together, and produce young like themselves. This distinction corresponds closely to the zoologists' definition of a species.

Zoologists use an internationally recognized system for naming species consisting of two-word scientific names, usually in Latin or Greek. The western diamondback rattlesnake is called *Crotalus atrox,* and the sidewinder *Crotalus cerastes. Crotalus* is the name of the genus (a group of very similar species); *atrox* or *cerastes* indicates the species in the genus. The same scientific names are recognized the world over. However, a species

This chart lists the phyla in two of the five kingdoms. The phylum Arthropoda makes up a high proportion of all invertebrate animals.

The main groups of animals alive today. Volumes that cover each major group are indicated below.

	ANIMALS Kingdom Animalia	SINGLE-CELLED LIFE Kingdom Protista

| Vertebrates/Chordates
Phylum Chordata | | Invertebrates
Numerous Phyla | |

Mammals Class Mammalia	Birds Class Aves	Reptiles Class Reptilia	Amphibians Class Amphibia	Fish Several classes	Insects, spiders, mollusks, spiny-skinned animals, worms	Single-Celled Life
Volumes 1–10	Volumes 11–20	Volumes 44–50	Volumes 41–43	Volumes 31–40	Volumes 21–30	Volume 21 (part)

Groups of Amphibians and Reptiles

may have been described and named at different times without the zoologists realizing it was one species.

Classification allows us to make statements about larger groups of animals. For example, all rattlesnakes are vipers—along with other vipers they are placed in the family Viperidae. All vipers are placed with all other snakes in the suborder Serpentes; snakes are related to lizards, which are in the suborder Sauria, and so these two groups combine to form the order Squamata in the class Reptilia.

An important point must be made about the current scientific knowledge of these animals. New discoveries are being made every day, from the biology of individual creatures to the finding and naming of new species. Our knowledge of the relationships among the different groups is changing constantly. In addition, the number of species known increases all the time, particularly in the light of the very latest DNA analysis techniques that are available to zoologists.

WHAT IS A REPTILE?

The reptiles form the class Reptilia. There are just over 8,000 species in total, and they are divided into four groups, or orders: the Testudines (turtles and tortoises), the Squamata (lizards, amphisbaenians, and snakes), the Crocodylia (crocodiles and alligators), and the Rhynchocephalia (tuataras). The numbers are unevenly divided among the orders, with the Squamata being the largest group in terms of numbers of species. It is also the most widespread group with almost global distribution. It is divided further into three suborders: the Amphisbaenia (amphisbaenians, or worm lizards), the Sauria (lizards), and the Serpentes (snakes).

Although reptiles are less conspicuous than many other animal groups, they form a unit within the system of biological classification that puts them on a par with other major groups such as insects, birds, and mammals.

Like fish, amphibians, birds, and mammals, reptiles are vertebrates (animals with a backbone). However, they obtain their body heat from outside sources (they are ectotherms) rather than producing it metabolically from their food. This ability separates them from birds and mammals, which are endothermic. They are separated from the fish and the amphibians by their reproductive biology: Reptile embryos are surrounded by three special membranes: the amnion, chorion, and allantois. The evolution of the "amniotic egg," as it is called, was a significant step and one that led subsequently to the evolution of birds and mammals.

Reptiles lay shelled eggs or produce live young depending on species. That means they are not closely tied to water, unlike most amphibians (although perversely some reptiles, such as crocodilians and sea turtles, have become aquatic as adults and have to come back to the land to lay their eggs, the very opposite of amphibians). In contrast to amphibians, reptiles are covered in dry, horny scales that are relatively impermeable to water. These two factors (their scales and their amniotic eggs) allowed them to move away from watery habitats and colonize the interiors of continents, even though some still favor wet or aquatic habitats.

⊕ *Representatives of reptile groups: tuatara (Sphenodon punctatus, order Rhyncocephala) (1); female false gharial (Tomistoma schlegelii, order Crocodylia) (2); worm lizard (order Squamata, suborder Amphisbaenia) (3); Alabama red-bellied turtle (Pseudemys alabamensis, order Testudines) (4); green tree python (Morelia viridis, order Squamata, suborder Serpentes) (5); Madagascan day gecko (Phelsuma laticauda, order Squamata, suborder Sauria) (6).*

Temperature Regulation

Understanding how reptiles operate at different temperatures is the key to understanding their behavior, biology, and ecology. Each species has a "preferred body temperature" at which they are best able to move around to hunt for and digest their food, to produce eggs or sperm, and so on. The temperature varies according to species but is often about 85 to 100°F (30–37°C). They may still be active at lower temperatures but they slow down, and at some point conditions will become too cold for them to move at all. This is known as the "critical lower temperature." If they have not found shelter at this point, they become stranded and are vulnerable to

5

6

predation. If the temperature continues to fall, they are at risk of freezing (they reach their "lethal minimum temperature"). The same thing happens with rising temperatures. Critical maximum temperatures are often quite close to preferred body temperatures, so even a small rise can spell trouble. The reptile must find a place away from the heat (in the shade, under a rock, or in a burrow) to keep its body from becoming overheated. Reptiles trapped in the sun (if they fall into a trench, for instance) succumb and die in minutes on hot days.

Reptiles living in different climates clearly need to use different strategies to maintain a suitable temperature. In the tropics they may need to do little by way of thermoregulation because the ambient temperature may be close to their optimum for much of the time. In cooler climates, such as North America, South Africa, and Europe, they can raise their body temperature during the warmest part of the day in spring and summer, perhaps by basking, but nighttime temperatures may be too cool for them on all but the warmest nights.

Species living in these climates tend to be diurnal, but depending on their locality, they may become nocturnal during midsummer. Of course, different species have different preferred body temperatures,

so even in the same locality some may be diurnal and some nocturnal. In winter none of them can reach their preferred temperature at any time of the day, and they need to retreat to a safe place and remain there in hibernation until the following spring.

At the other extreme, reptiles living in very hot places are often active at night and seek shelter during the day. Another advantage is that they can reduce the risk of predation by daytime hunters such as birds of prey (but not by nocturnal predators, of course). Where conditions are too harsh, they may retreat underground for days or even weeks at a time to "sit out" the worst excesses of the climate before returning to the surface (this is known as estivation). In practice, most reptiles that estivate usually do so in order to avoid extreme dryness rather

⊕ *Many reptiles need to bask in the sun to reach their body's preferred temperature. In central Oman a spiny-tailed lizard,* Uromastyx aegyptia microlepis, *stretches out on a rock to warm up.*

⊖ *Right: A chart demonstrating the main lines of reptilian evolution. The four subclasses of reptiles (Euryapsida, Anapsida, Diapsida, and Synapsida) are distinguished by the arched recesses, or apses, in the skull behind the eye sockets.*

Below right: Anapsida (1) have no apses, and today they are represented by the turtles and tortoises. Synapsida (2) have one apse, and this line led to the evolution of mammals. Diapsids (3), with two apses, included the now extinct dinosaurs and are represented today by all other reptile groups apart from turtles and tortoises. The Euryapsids (4) had one apse high on the skull and are represented by the now extinct marine reptiles of the Mesozoic.

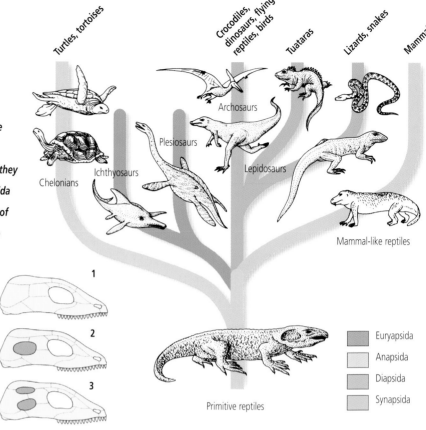

than heat, and they tend to be species that normally rely on water, for example, crocodilians and freshwater turtles.

Maintaining the correct body temperature by thermoregulation takes several forms in reptiles. Species that live in open environments shuttle backward and forward between areas of sun and areas of shade. Some of them are dark in color so that they absorb heat more quickly. They may also flatten or orient their body in a particular way to help absorb heat more quickly: American fence lizards, *Sceloporus* species, side-blotched lizards in the genus *Uta*, and European vipers, *Vipera* species, are good examples.

Forest dwellers have less opportunity to bask, but they can move into small open areas where the sun gets through or move up into the canopy. Aquatic species, such as crocodilians and turtles, have limited opportunities to control their body temperatures and must often "make do" with whatever temperature the water happens to be; most of them come from warmer climates where typical temperatures are suitable. Crocodiles, alligators, and freshwater turtles may "haul out" for long periods to bask on the riverbank or on logs or rocks that stick out. Sea turtles do not usually bask, except perhaps at the water's surface, and so they are restricted to the tropics. Burrowing species, such as the worm lizards, may be able

to move up and down through the levels of their tunnels; but by and large they do not actively thermoregulate, and they are sometimes known as "thermal conformers."

Origins of Reptiles

Reptiles evolved from four-legged amphibians about 350 million years ago. However, species that would pinpoint their exact origins have not been positively identified from fossil records. They are known to have laid amniotic eggs, which was a significant development. By 310 million years ago the early land-dwelling animals that laid amniotic eggs split into two branches, one that would lead to the mammals and the other to reptiles and birds. The implications of this division are, perhaps surprisingly, that birds are more closely related to reptiles than to mammals—some scientists even maintain that they are reptiles.

⊖ *A scene from an early Jurassic landscape shows the diversity of reptilian life. A pterosaur, Rhamphorhyncus (1); a stegosaur, Kentrosaurus (2); theropod dinosaurs, Elaphrosaurus (3) and Ceratosaurus (4); sauropod dinosaurs, Dicraeosaurus (5), and Brachiosaurus (6).*

By the end of the Triassic Period (about 208 million years ago) the oldest lineages of reptiles that we know today had appeared. They were the early chelonians, or shelled reptiles (turtles and tortoises), the crocodilians, and the rhynchocephalians (the ancestors of the tuataras). The lizards, worm lizards, and snakes came later, first appearing during the Jurassic Period about 208 to 144 million years ago. The worm lizards are thought to be the most recently evolved of the major groups. Many other branches of the reptile lineage led to evolutionary dead ends but only after they had been highly successful for very long periods of time before eventually dying out.

Form and Function

Compared with birds or mammals, living reptiles form a diverse group. There are species with and without shells. Some have four limbs, some have two, and some have none. All are covered in scales, but the scales can be massive, knobby, and stonelike or tiny, granular, and silky to the touch. Compare a snapping turtle or an alligator with an anole lizard or a gecko to get an idea of the wide range of forms and sizes in the order. The sizes, shapes, and colors of reptiles are not there to help us tell one species from another: They have been finetuned through the evolutionary process to help each species adapt to its particular place in the scheme of things. Even small groups of closely related species contain very diverse species occupying different ecological niches.

We know that stout snakes with short tails are likely to be slow-moving, burrowing reptiles, and that long, thin ones with long tails are likely to be fast-moving, terrestrial types (unless they have prehensile tails, in which case they will be climbers). Flattened turtles with streamlined shells are aquatic, while species with domed shells and elephantlike feet are terrestrial, and so on.

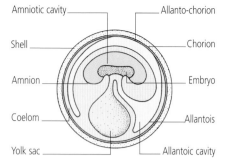

Amniotic cavity — Allanto-chorion
Shell — Chorion
Amnion — Embryo
Coelom — Allantois
Yolk sac — Allantoic cavity

⊖ *Developing egg, showing layers of membrane between shell and embryo. The partly fused chorion and allantois on the inner surface of the shell are supplied with blood vessels, enabling the embryo to breathe through pores in the shell. The allantois also acts as a repository for the embryo's waste products. The amnion is a fluid-filled sac around the embryo that keeps it from drying out. The yolk sac contains the embryonic food supply, rich in protein and fats. Eggs of this type, such as those of birds, are called cleidoic ("closed-box") eggs, since apart from respiration and some absorption of water from the environment, they are self-sufficient. Water absorption by the eggs of many reptiles, especially the softer-shelled types, is higher than by birds' eggs.*

⊖ *Reptilian hearts. In most reptiles the chambers of the ventricles are incompletely separated (1). In crocodilians complete separation exists, although there is a small connection, the foramen of Panizza, between the outlet vessels (2). Even in the unseparated ventricle a system of valves and blood pressure differences ensures that there is little mixing of arterial and venous blood under normal conditions. In all reptiles, however, the potential exists to shunt the blood from one side of the heart to the other. This helps them adapt, especially aquatic animals, since blood can be recycled when breathing is interrupted.*

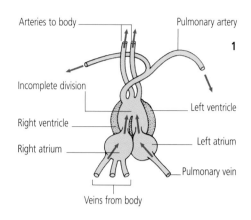

Arteries to body — Pulmonary artery
1
Incomplete division — Left ventricle
Right ventricle — Left atrium
Right atrium — Pulmonary vein
Veins from body

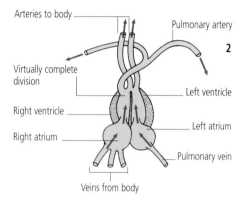

Arteries to body — Pulmonary artery
2
Virtually complete division — Left ventricle
Right ventricle — Left atrium
Right atrium — Pulmonary vein
Veins from body

Within several families of lizards there has been a tendency to lose limbs, which is also related to lifestyle. The skinks are a particularly good example of "adaptive radiation"—the process by which related species evolve in different ways to suit different conditions. Skinks range from tiny, legless, burrowing forms through elongated, grass-dwelling species with tiny reduced limbs to chunky, heavy-bodied, terrestrial forms.

Coloration is usually related to defense. Cryptic, or disguised, species are colored to match their surroundings, and other species have disruptive geometric markings that help break up their outline. Some species are so well camouflaged that they are nearly impossible to make out even when you know where they are. Other reptiles, however, are brightly colored to warn that they are venomous. On the other hand, there are species that are harmless but also brightly colored to fool predators into thinking that they are venomous (known as Batesian mimicry). Some camouflaged species have brightly colored patches or extensions to their body that they can flash when they want to display to other members of their own species or to deter potential predators.

Who Lives Where and Why?

Because they are dependent on temperature, reptiles are most at home in tropical and subtropical regions, with the greatest numbers of species and individuals occurring in the tropical rain forests of Central and South America, West and Central Africa, and Southeast Asia. Farther away from the tropics toward the poles the numbers fall dramatically. Species that do not have the ability to thermoregulate, such as burrowing and aquatic reptiles, are even more restricted to warm places.

Superimposed on this pattern are the historical events that have affected the way in which reptiles have been able to spread across the globe. At about the time they were diversifying most rapidly, the landmasses and "supercontinents" were changing shape through continental drift. Areas that had been connected were breaking apart, while in other places landmasses collided. Evolving reptiles were "passengers" on these landmasses; and lacking the ability to cover large tracts of water (with the obvious exception of the sea turtles), they became isolated in some places but were presented with opportunities to expand in others.

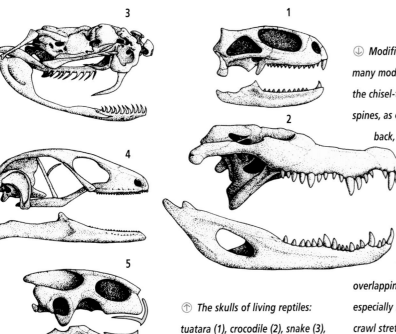

① The skulls of living reptiles: tuatara (1), crocodile (2), snake (3), lizard (4), and turtle (5).

⊕ *Modifications of the skin. The skin, particularly the epidermis, shows many modifications in reptiles. It can be raised up into tubercles, as in the chisel-toothed lizard, Ceratophora stoddari (1), or into defensive spines, as on the tails of certain lizards. It can form crests on the neck, back, or tail, often better developed in the male and perhaps helping in sexual recognition, as in Lyriocephalus scutatus (2). The rattlesnake's rattle (3), made up of interlocking horny segments, is a unique epidermal structure; a new segment is formed at each molt, but the end segment tends to break off when the rattle gets very long. In most snakes the underbody scales are enlarged to form a series of wide, overlapping plates that assist in locomotion, especially in forms such as boas that can crawl stretched out almost straight. The modified scales, or lamellae, on the toe pads of geckos (4) have fine bristles (setae) that allow them to climb smooth surfaces.*

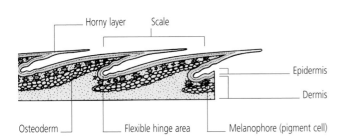

Horny layer | Scale

Epidermis

Dermis

Osteoderm | Flexible hinge area | Melanophore (pigment cell)

① *Cross-sectional diagram of the skin of a slowworm. All anguimorphs such as this are heavily armored, having mostly nonoverlapping scales with underlying osteoderms.*

"Older" lineages (those that appeared early on) were able to spread onto most landmasses and travel with them. Some of them subsequently thrived and became widespread (the geckos, for example), while the success of others diminished as more adaptable groups ousted them. For the "newer" families, however, some options were closed because they were already isolated by the time they appeared. That is why there are no vipers in Australasia and no monitor lizards in the Americas.

Isolated island groups are often very poor in reptile species, but their patterns of colonization and speciation (species formation) are especially interesting to biologists because they can add to our understanding of the processes of evolution and natural selection. The most obvious example is the Galápagos archipelago. Reptiles first spread to places like this accidentally (and perhaps only on one or two occasions), possibly by "rafting" on mats of floating vegetation.

Reproduction

Unlike the amphibians, reptiles have internal fertilization. The male introduces the sperm directly into the female's reproductive tract through the cloaca, which is the opening for the digestive and reproductive systems. In all reptiles except the tuataras males have copulatory organs. In lizards, snakes, and worm lizards they are paired and are called the hemipenes. There is usually competition among males for access to females, which can take various forms. In species that use visual clues for communication, such as some lizards, males often display crests, frills, or brightly colored parts of their anatomy to

⊕ A clutch of eggs laid by a female milksnake hatches out. Most snakes lay eggs, but other reptiles, including some snakes, are live-bearers. Reproductive patterns are often determined by lifestyle and habitat.

attract mates and to advertise their ownership of territory. Color change can also be involved, most famously in chameleons. The courtship process in many species, especially secretive ones such as skinks and worm lizards, is poorly known, but chemical communication almost certainly plays an important part.

Reproductive cycles vary greatly according to species and where they live. Some tropical species breed all year around, while some from colder climates breed only once every two or three years. Tuataras breed only every five or more years. Most temperate species breed in the spring and summer, but again there is some variation.

Reptiles may lay eggs or give birth to live young. This is an evolutionary "decision" with important tradeoffs. Laying eggs frees the female to continue feeding and may enable her to produce a second clutch quickly; on the other hand, the eggs are vulnerable to predation and are at the mercy of the elements. Giving birth to live young enables the female to care for her developing embryos more effectively because she is carrying them around with her, but it is an added burden for several months. The "choice" she makes (in evolutionary terms) will depend on factors such as climate and lifestyle.

Superimposed on this, however, is an ancestral element: Reptiles in some families seem "locked into" a particular reproductive mode (for example, all pythons lay eggs, but nearly all boas give birth to live young). The crocodilians, turtles, and tuataras do not seem to have evolved the facility to give birth—they lay eggs, which is the "ancestral mode" for all reptiles. Among lizards and snakes most lay eggs, but a significant proportion are live-bearers. Many aquatic snakes, including the sea snakes, give birth because finding a suitable place to lay their eggs presents a problem (although some species, notably the sea kraits, come ashore to lay eggs). Worm lizards are all egg layers as far as is known, but the natural history of many of these obscure reptiles remains a mystery.

Food and Feeding

Among them reptiles eat just about anything organic. There are divisions along taxonomic lines, however. All snakes are carnivorous, for instance, although their prey can vary from ants to antelopes. Crocodilians are also carnivorous—their prey ranges from insects to large mammals such as zebras and wildebeests. Worm lizards are probably all carnivorous too and feed largely on burrowing insects such as ants and termites, but the larger species also take small vertebrates, including lizards. Lizards feed on a wide variety of items— many eat insects, but many others are herbivores. Large monitors are ferocious predators of vertebrates such as other lizards, birds, and mammals. Marine and freshwater turtles eat animal and plant material depending on species, and some eat both. Land turtles tend to be herbivores but are not averse to eating animals when they can catch them, which is not very often. A number of reptiles, perhaps more than we realize, eat carrion as a sideline.

Methods of finding and overcoming food are equally diverse. Finding and catching plant material is not very hard, although plants are well known for producing toxins to deter grazers and browsers. Many reptiles are amazingly oblivious to spines and bitter substances, and can eat plant species that other herbivores reject.

Catching animal prey takes a number of different forms. Many are "sit-and-wait" predators, setting themselves up in a likely place and waiting for prey to blunder past. American horned lizards, *Phrynosoma* species, and Australian thorny devils, *Moloch horridus*, position themselves next to ant trails and simply mop up

the ants as they walk past. Overpowering larger prey—especially if it can fight back—calls for more cunning and specialized equipment. The ultimate weapon is the evolution of venom in some snakes, which enables them to dispense death in the blink of an eye even to animals many times their own size.

Classification of Species

Compared with other groups of zoology, the naming and reclassification of reptiles seems to be always in a state of change. In 2003, for example, there were 59 new species described, 3 subspecies were elevated to full species, and 18 species were suppressed (because it turned out that they had been named twice). In 2002 there were 60 new species, in 2001 80 new species were named, and 72 new species were described in 2000. In just four years, then, 271 completely new species were added to the reptiles. In the same period there were few, if any, new birds or mammals. What is more, scientists are constantly reclassifying and renaming existing species to try to represent more accurately the relationships between them. This can make life difficult for those studying or writing about reptiles.

Many new reptile species are discovered in places that have hardly been explored from a herpetological point of view, such as Madagascar. Other species belong to groups that are hard to find or difficult to work with (or both), such as the blind and thread snakes, Leptotyphlopidae and Typhlopidae. Others are still turning up in parts of the world where herpetologists have been working for years and belong to conspicuous groups of reptiles. The reptile lists of South Africa and Australia, for example, have grown significantly in the last 10 years or so—by 20 percent in South Africa, an average of one new species every 44 days!

↩ *The Galápagos Islands are home to some of the most unusual reptiles, including the marine iguanas, Amblyrhynchus cristatus. They are the only lizards that enter the sea and feed on seaweed.*

15

Declining Species

Until 200 years ago the Galápagos Islands were home to hundreds of thousands of giant tortoises. During the 19th century visiting whaling ships began to collect the tortoises to stock their holds with fresh meat. They left behind a number of destructive, introduced mammals—rats, cats, pigs, and goats—that preyed on the tortoises' eggs and young or competed with them for food. By the mid-20th century three of the original 14 subspecies of giant tortoise were extinct. Only four subspecies are considered to be safe from extinction. Six out of a total of seven marine turtle species are classed as Endangered or Critically Endangered (IUCN) as are seven of just 22 surviving species of crocodilians.

According to the IUCN 21 species of reptiles have become extinct in recent times. Sixteen of them lived on islands. Island species are especially vulnerable because their environment is easily affected by human impacts, especially the introduction of predatory animals. On Round Island in the Indian Ocean every native reptile species is extinct or on the brink of extinction, while Mauritius has lost eight species.

Not all the news is bad, however. The surviving Galápagos tortoises are being bred successfully in captivity, goats and rats have been eliminated on some islands, and the vegetation is beginning to recover. The Jamaican iguana, *Cyclura collei*, was believed extinct since the 1940s but turned up in small numbers in 1990 on a

Reptiles as Pets

Reptiles have become popular pets. Species available range from small geckos to huge pythons and the common boa (*Boa constrictor*). Many are now being selectively bred to give the enthusiast a wide selection of color and pattern forms. Their care varies greatly according to the species, so always seek the advice of the vendor, and consult a specialist book for the relevant information.

Captive-bred animals should be obtained wherever possible. There are a number of reasons for this. First, they will be better adapted to captivity than wild ones and will therefore calm down sooner and be more inclined to accept an unnatural diet. Second, they are likely to be free from parasites and infections that often plague specimens captured from the wild. Third, the fact that they were produced in captivity means that they are an adaptable species. Finally, many wild reptile populations are under threat, and to encourage trade in them is irresponsible. Many species are protected internationally, nationally, or locally, and you may be breaking the law by keeping them. Similarly, collecting species from national or state parks is not allowed.

Accommodation

Accommodation can range from plastic containers for the smallest species (or for rearing juveniles of some of the larger species) to huge, room-sized cages that will

⊕ *Green iguanas lie trussed up ready for sale at a market in Guyana. These animals are destined for the cooking pot; their flesh is often used in stews and curries in that part of the world.*

be necessary to house the large constricting snakes or large, active lizards such as iguanas and monitors. As a rule, however, beginners are advised to avoid any large, active species. Venomous snakes and lizards do not make good pets either, for obvious reasons.

Environment

Background reading about the natural history of your chosen species will provide clues to its requirements. Heating of some sort will probably be necessary depending on the species you keep and where you live. Diurnal lizards and snakes prefer an overhead light source such as a heat lamp or spotlight because they are used to basking in the sun. Others fare better if a gentle heat is applied under their cage by means of a heat mat or heat strip. The best plan is to arrange the heating at one end of the cage only: That will create a thermal gradient, and the reptile will be able to move from one part of the cage to another to take advantage of different temperatures.

In addition, many lizards and turtles require a source of ultraviolet light because it enables them to synthesize vitamin D, which they need in order to absorb calcium into their skeleton. In the wild they would obtain vitamin D from sunlight, but in captivity special lights, together with dietary supplements, are often necessary to provide the correct nutritional balance. Lighting is not normally required for most of the more popular snakes such as corn snakes because in nature they shun the light and are most active in the evening and at night. Garter snakes, however, do like to bask.

Some species are very sensitive to humidity, and it is important to make sure that they are neither too damp nor too dry. Some species are particularly susceptible to shedding problems if they are kept too dry. If their skin becomes dry or comes away in many pieces, that is a sure sign they are being kept in conditions that are too dry. Clearly, freshwater turtles require an area of water, and some species can be kept in totally aquatic accommodation such as an aquarium; but most will need an area where they can crawl out to bask under a light source.

Feeding

There are almost as many types of reptile food as there are reptiles. However, it is best to choose a species whose diet is easily catered to in captivity. Insectivorous lizards, snakes, and turtles will usually eat crickets, which can be bought from pet stores, or you may be able to collect enough insects, at least during the summer.

Earthworms are another good source of food for species that will eat them. Many snakes require vertebrate food, of which the most convenient is rodents, which can be bought frozen and then thawed out as required. Again, captive-bred individuals are more likely to accept food that has been stored in this way; wild snakes often insist on having, at best, freshly killed prey, which is not always convenient (or legal).

remote hillside. Eggs have been collected, a captive-breeding program is underway, and young iguanas will be released into the wild once they are no longer vulnerable.

Cause for Concern

Despite these measures hundreds of reptile species may disappear over the next century. Habitat destruction through agricultural development, urbanization, mineral extraction, erosion, and pollution, is the most important cause. On top of this thousands of reptiles are killed by traffic on the roads every day, and several populations have been lost through the flooding of valleys for hydro-electrical projects. Reptiles are also hunted for food, their eggs, or the pet trade. Sea turtles enjoy total protection throughout the world but poachers still take adults and eggs in many of the poorer parts of the world, and wild crocodilians are still hunted illegally for their skins.

Not only rare species are affected. Some species that were widespread a few decades ago are becoming scarce. Many people will grow up without ever seeing a wild lizard, snake, or turtle. The challenge for the future will be to find ways to reconcile the human race's need to expand and feed itself with the preservation of the wild places needed by reptiles and other animals.

Sphenodon punctatus

Common name Tuataras

Scientific names *Sphenodon punctatus, S. guntheri*

Family   Sphenodontidae

Order   Rhynchocephalia

Size   From 20 in (50 cm) to 31 in (80 cm); males larger than females

Key features Body squat; color of adults olive-green, gray, or black with a speckling of gray, yellow, or white; newly hatched animals are brown or gray with pink tinges; head has a pink shield and striped throat; sometimes distinctive light patches occur on the body and tail

Habits   Nocturnal burrowers

Breeding   Egg layers; average clutch size from 6 to 10; incubation period about 11–15 months

Diet   Invertebrates such as beetles, crickets, and spiders; also the eggs and chicks of seabirds; frogs, lizards, and young tuataras also eaten occasionally

Habitat   Low forest and scrub usually associated with colonies of burrowing seabirds

Distribution About 33 small islands and rock stacks off the coast of New Zealand

Status   *S. guntheri* is listed as Vulnerable (IUCN); *S. punctatus* has a very limited range

Similar species None

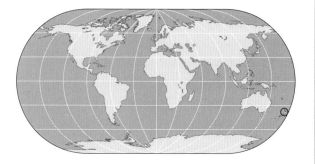

Tuataras

Sphenodon punctatus
and *S. guntheri*

The tuataras are the sole survivors of a group of reptiles that have existed for about 220 million years. They are found only on some small islands around the coast of New Zealand.

THE TWO SPECIES OF TUATARAS, *Sphenodon guntheri* and *S. punctatus,* are found on offshore islets around the New Zealand coast. They are the only members of the order Rhynchocephalia (recently renamed the Sphenodontia in some publications). They belong to a branch of reptiles called the Lepidosauria (scaly reptiles), which also contains the squamates (lizards, snakes, and worm lizards).

The other reptilian branches are the Archosauria, containing the crocodilians and a number of extinct lines such as the dinosaurs, and the Chelonia (turtles and tortoises). Strangely, the Archosauria also includes the birds, making them more closely related to reptiles than to mammals. Similarities between the skulls of tuataras and crocodilians led to early classification systems placing them close together in evolutionary terms, but the similarities are now believed to be coincidental.

Early Reptiles

The rhynchocephalians were among the first reptiles to appear, at around the same time as the crocodiles (and the dinosaurs), even though they have no direct connection to them. The tuataras, therefore, have an ancestry that goes back to the Triassic Period about 220 million years ago at the beginning of the "Age of the Dinosaurs." Tuataras are sometimes referred to as "living fossils," but it should be stressed that it was their ancestors that lived at the same time as the dinosaurs—the tuataras as we know them today arrived later.

Fossil rhynchocephalians have been found in many parts of the world, including Africa, Madagascar, Europe, and South America. At the time they evolved, the southern landmasses

⊕ *In the wild tuataras are mostly nocturnal. They make their homes in burrows and emerge at night to prey on insects of various types and occasionally the eggs of seabirds.*

were all joined into the supercontinent of Gondwanaland, and they were able to spread out and diversify across a wide region. Twenty-four genera have been identified from fossils, and no doubt there are plenty more waiting to be found. Others were never lucky enough to become fossilized. As the landmass broke up into the continents, rhynchocephalians became extinct throughout the world until by 60 million years ago they had completely disappeared, except on the relatively small landmass that became New Zealand. Their survival there was due to New Zealand's early separation from the rest of the landmasses and consequently its lack of large predators. So they lived

an untroubled life in splendid isolation until the arrival of humans about 1,000 years ago. That event heralded their disappearance from the mainland and several of the larger offshore islands, mainly due to introduced animals (although tuatara remains have been found in kitchen middens of the earliest inhabitants, suggesting that they were eaten). Today they live only on about 30 small islands, mostly less than 25 acres (10 ha) in area. Five of them are in the Cook Straits between New Zealand's North and South Islands, and the rest are in the Gulf of Hauraki and the Bay of Plenty off North Island's northeast coast.

The tuatara was first described in 1831 and placed in the Agamidae. Historically, tuataras were thought to be lizards and were given a variety of names until 1867, when a scientist named Dr. Albert Gunther, working at the British Museum, recognized their link with the rhynchocephalians (which were thought to have been extinct for a long time). The tuatara was named *Sphenodon punctatus*. (*Sphenodon* means "wedge toothed.") Then in 1989 Dr. Charles Daugherty, working at Victoria Museum in Wellington, concluded that there were two species involved. The new one, from North Brothers Island, was named *S. guntheri* after Dr. Gunther. The Maoris, who were the original colonizers of New Zealand, gave them the common name tuatara, which means "peaks on the back," a reference to the jagged crest on the back and tail of both species.

What Makes Them Different?

Apart from their skulls, tuataras have several characteristics that set them apart from other reptiles. Unlike any lizards, they have a single row of teeth in the lower jaw that fits between two rows of teeth in the upper jaw. The arrangement enables the tuataras to grind and shear tough foodstuffs, such as the outer skeletons of some of their insect prey. The teeth are fused to the upper edge of the jawbone (and are known as acrodont). As a result, tuataras have only a limited ability to replace worn-out teeth, so those of older animals are

often worn completely level with the jaw. Most lizards, on the other hand, have pleurodont teeth, a condition in which they are loosely attached to the inside surface of the jawbones, although members of the Agamidae also have acrodont teeth. A second difference is that male tuataras do not have an external copulatory organ. Instead, sperm is transferred from the male's cloaca directly to that of the female. Tuataras lack external openings to their ears, while the majority of lizards have them.

Tuataras are brown, olive, or reddish brown in color with no distinct markings other than a light speckling of white or yellow. They have a crest consisting of a raised ridge topped with a row of toothlike scales, which is higher and larger in males than in females. They grow to 20 to 30 inches in length (50–76 cm) with a maximum weight of about 2.2 pounds (1kg). Males are larger than females, which are significantly lighter and have narrower heads.

Tuataras and Birds

Tuataras live in coastal forests at densities between 3,000 and 5,000 in every acre (1,300–2000 per ha). They live in burrows that they can dig themselves, but on some islands they also make use of burrows belonging to a variety of species of seabirds that use the islands as nesting sites. The main species are the common diving petrel, *Pelecanoides*

A Third Eye

When tuataras hatch, they have a translucent scale on top of their head. It covers a well-developed structure resembling an "eye" that is situated between two large bones on top of the skull (the parietal bones). A similar structure is found in some lizards, but it is most obvious in young tuataras.

The function of the "eye" is poorly known; but it has a lens and a retina, and it is connected to the brain. It is thought to be sensitive to light but not capable of producing an image, and many scientists think that it helps the animals regulate their exposure to the sun and control their daily activity rhythms.

urinatrix, known locally as mutton birds, and fairy prions, *Pachyptila turtur*.

Tuataras are nocturnal. They search for their prey by sight, mostly in the area immediately around their burrows. The presence of the seabirds and their guano encourages a high density of scavenging invertebrates, especially the giant crickets known locally as wetas, which the tuataras eat. They also eat the eggs and the young of the nesting birds occasionally, along with lizards and smaller members of their own species.

Life in the Slow Lane

Because they live in a cool climate, tuataras have evolved a slow metabolic rate. They maintain a lower body temperature than most other reptiles and are active when their body temperature reaches 45°F (7°C) or more. However, they sometimes bask in the sun at the entrance to their burrows, when their body temperature can reach 80°F (27°C). Their preferred body temperature seems to be about 60°F (15°C).

The effect of the low metabolic rate is to slow down their development and growth and to prolong their lives: Tuataras only become sexually mature after about 10 years old, and they continue growing until they are 20 to 35 years old. They may breed until they are at least 60 years old, possibly for much longer, although more research will be needed to confirm this. So far, captives have lived for 77 years, but a life span of 100 years is not unlikely.

Every other aspect of their lives moves at a slower pace too. For example, females only

ⓐ *A female tuatara watches the approach of a male* Sphenodon punctatus *in a tree on Stephen's Island, New Zealand.*

produce eggs every two to five years. The eggs take up to three years to develop in the female's ovaries, and it takes seven months more for the shell to form around them. Their incubation period is the longest of any reptile.

Breeding

The mating season coincides with the southern summer (January to March). At this time the males become more territorial and display to each other and to females by raising their crests. After mating, the females ovulate but do not lay their eggs until the following spring when the shell has been formed. Then they migrate to open areas where they can dig tunnels in which to lay their eggs. The tunnels are about 8 inches (20 cm) in length, and the females defend them for a few days after laying to keep other females from digging in the same place and disturbing their eggs.

Tuataras lay 10 to 15 soft-shelled, elongated eggs. Incubation takes from 11 to 15 months, but that includes a period during the winter when the embryo's development is arrested. Eggs laid in captivity and incubated at a constant temperature develop more quickly. As in turtles, crocodilians, and some lizards, for example, the leopard gecko, *Eublepharus macularius,* the hatchlings' sex depends on the temperature at which the eggs develop: Higher temperatures produce males, while lower temperatures produce females.

Just before they hatch, the eggs absorb water. They swell, and their shells become taut. The embryo develops a small "egg tooth" on its snout, which it uses to slit the shell. The egg tooth falls off about two weeks after hatching.

Defense

Adult tuataras have little need to defend themselves because they have no predators. But juveniles are vulnerable to predation by larger tuataras as well as by owls, hawks, and kingfishers, so they live in small burrows that they dig for themselves or under rocks or logs.

Tuataras can shed part of their tail, a process known as autotomy. The tail breaks across a fracture plane in one of the vertebrae rather than at the junction of two, and the bone, nerves, and blood vessels all break cleanly. The discarded part of the tail continues to twitch to attract the attention of the predator while the tuatara escapes. The stump heals quickly: Four pairs of muscle bundles emerge from the stump immediately after the break, and they gradually bend inward, sealing off the nerve ends and blood vessels to prevent the loss of blood and further damage. A conical scar forms, skin grows over it, and the stump slowly elongates over a period of several weeks. The vertebrae of the original tail are replaced by rods of cartilage, and new blood vessels and nerves extend into the new section. Scientists assume that most of the widespread tail damage is due to fighting—attacks by predators could probably not account for the high proportion of tuataras with regrown tails.

Conservation Program

Tuataras have few natural enemies on their isolated islands. The main threats are from introduced predators such as dogs, cats, and rats, and from habitat destruction. There are no islands where rats and tuataras coexist—islands on which there were once good populations of tuataras that have since disappeared all have introduced rats on them. On some islands all the tuatara populations consist only of adults, which is worrying because it suggests that none of the young are surviving. On the other hand, tuataras coexist well with seabirds and are most successful where there is a healthy population of petrels, prions, and shearwaters.

Tuataras have been totally protected by law since 1953. All the islands on which they currently live are small and have steep cliffs that make landing by boat difficult. In addition, landing is restricted to scientists and conservationists who have special permission.

Recently a program to breed tuataras in captivity has been developed and seems to be producing good results. Eggs are collected from healthy populations and hatched under controlled conditions. The hatchlings are then

① *The common green gecko,* Naultinus elegans, *is endemic to New Zealand. As its name suggests, it is the most familiar green gecko on the North Island. It can be green, yellow, or patterned with both colors.*

Reptile Neighbors

Very few reptiles managed to reach New Zealand before it became separated from the main southern landmass. Before humans arrived, the tuatara would have been the dominant reptile species throughout the country. Nowadays the two main islands (North Island and South Island) have representatives of two lizard families but no snakes, turtles, or crocodilians at all.

The 40 or so species of lizards belong to the Gekkonidae and the Scincidae in roughly equal numbers. All 18 of the geckos are in the genera *Hoplodactylus* and *Naultinus*. They are endemic to New Zealand, and unusually, they are all live-bearers (there are only a handful of other live-bearing geckos in the world). The skinks are slightly more numerous, with 22 species all in the genus *Oligosoma*. They are also live-bearers, with the sole exception of *O. suteri* from Great Barrier Island, North Island, which lays eggs.

released on islands where former populations were wiped out. Since 1995 three islands have been cleared of invasive rats, and juveniles have been reintroduced. The plan will be judged a success when the introduced animals produce a second generation of tuataras.

Altogether it is believed that there are over 60,000 common tuataras distributed among 29 islands, so their future is relatively secure. The Brothers Island tuatara, *Sphenodon guntheri*, however, only occurs on the North Brothers Island in Marlborough Sound. The total population is about 400 animals. Although they are quite safe at present, they are vulnerable to accidental introduction of rats and to habitat destruction, especially by fire.

LIZARDS

Recent figures put the number of lizard species at 4,713—just over 57 percent of all reptile species. Lizard classification at the family level is currently unsatisfactory, with a number of different systems in use. For the purpose of this volume they are divided into 20 families, but some authorities recognize more or fewer. In particular, the Iguanidae is sometimes divided into eight separate families instead of the one listed here.

Almost everywhere in the world (except the Arctic or Antarctic regions) lizards are likely to be the most conspicuous reptiles. The geckos that scurry across the walls and ceilings of restaurants in Southeast Asia, the spiny and side-blotched lizards that scamper from rock to rock in the American Southwest, and the colorful wall lizards that grace the hillsides, walls, and ruins of the Mediterranean region are proof that lizards can succeed in making a living in a variety of places and habitats.

Many lizards are highly visual in their communication with each other and can also be very colorful. In Africa brilliantly colored male agamas bask and display on prominent rocks, bobbing blue or red heads at each other. And in the Caribbean region small, colorful anole lizards live in and around gardens, hotel grounds, and even airports, flashing colorful dewlaps at each other like tiny semaphore flags. All of them are hard to miss.

Lizards are among the most well studied of all reptiles. An observer can sit quietly and watch the whole soap opera that is lizard life unfolding as individuals display, fight, mate, eat, and get eaten. The colonial existence of the side-blotched lizard, *Uta stansburiana*, for example, has been thoroughly explored, and many unsuspected and fascinating facts have come to light. However, other lizards lead more secretive lives and are poorly known. Many tropical species are hardly studied at all and may be known from just a handful of specimens.

Extreme Sizes

The largest lizard is generally accepted to be the Komodo dragon, *Varanus komodoensis* from a group of small islands in Indonesia. Males of the species average about

7.5 feet (2.3 m) in length and weigh about 130 pounds (59 kg). The largest specimen to be reliably measured was 10.3 feet (3.1 m) long and weighed 365 pounds (166 kg). It died in 1933 and is on display at the Tilden Regional Park in Berkeley, California. Female Komodo dragons are significantly smaller than males, averaging about 65 percent of their length and perhaps half their weight. A related lizard, Salvadori's monitor, *Varanus salvadorii*, is actually longer than the Komodo dragon and measures up to 15.6 feet (4.75 m) in length. It is a more slender species, however, and its tail accounts for nearly three-quarters of its length, so it is nowhere near as bulky.

At the other extreme many small lizards measure less than 3 inches (7.5 cm). The smallest species is the Jaragua dwarf gecko, *Sphaerodactylus ariasae*. It lives among leaf litter on an island near the Dominican Republic in the West Indies. This tiny creature is just 1.4 inches (3.6 cm) long, including its tail. It is not surprising that it remained unknown until 2001. Its length is one-hundredth that of the Komodo dragon, and the whole lizard is shorter than

↑ → From giant to midget of the lizard world. Above: At 7.5 to 10 feet (2.3–3 m) long the Komodo dragon, Varanus komodoensis from Indonesia, is the largest lizard. At the other extreme the minuscule chameleon, Brookesia peyrierasi (right), is small enough to sit on a person's thumb.

Who's Who among the Lizards?

Order Squamata (suborder Sauria)

Family Agamidae: 49 genera, about 430 species of agamas, dragon lizards, or chisel-toothed lizards, including the red-headed rock agama, *Agama agama*, and the thorny devil, *Moloch horridus*

Family Chamaeleonidae: 6 genera, about 131 species of chameleons and dwarf chameleons, including panther chameleon, *Furcifer pardalis*, African dwarf chameleons, *Bradypodion* sp.

Family Iguanidae: 44 genera, about 892 species of iguanas, basilisks, collared lizards, anoles, and lava lizards, including green iguana, *Iguana iguana*, plumed basilisk, *Basiliscus plumifrons*, American horned lizards, *Phrynosoma* sp.

Family Gekkonidae: about 75 genera, 910 species of "typical" geckos, including tokay, *Gekko gecko*, day geckos, *Phelsuma* sp., ashy gecko, *Sphaerodactylus elegans*

Family Diplodactylidae: 14 genera, 115 species of "southern" geckos, including Australian leaf-tailed geckos, *Phyllurus* species, golden-tailed gecko, *Diplodactylus taenicauda*

Family Pygopodidae: 7 genera, 35 species of flap-footed lizards, including Burton's snake lizard, *Lialis burtoni*

Family Eublepharidae: 6 genera, 22 species of eyelid geckos, including leopard gecko, *Eublepharis macularius*, and western banded gecko, *Coleonyx variegatus*

Family Teiidae: 9 genera, 120 species of tegus, whiptails, racerunners, and related lizards, including black tegu, *Tupinambis teguixin*, desert grassland whiptail, *Cnemidophorus uniparens*

Family Gymnophthalmidae: 34 genera, 179 species of spectacled lizards, including white spectacled lizard, *Gymnophthalmus leucomystax*

Family Lacertidae: 26 genera, 279 species of wall, green, jeweled, and related lizards, including viviparous lizard, *Lacerta vivipara*, common wall lizard, *Podarcis muralis*

Family Xantusiidae: 3 genera, 26 species of night lizards, including desert night lizard, *Xantusia vigilis*

Family Scincidae: about 115–124 genera, about 1,400 species of skinks, including monkey-tailed skink, *Corucia zebrata*, five-lined skink, *Eumeces fasciatus*

Family Gerrhosauridae: 6 genera, 32 species of plated lizards, including giant plated lizard, *Gerrhosaurus validus*

Family Cordylidae: 4 genera, 55 species of girdle-tailed lizards, including black-girdled lizard, *Cordylus niger*

Family Dibamidae: 2 genera, 10 species of blind lizards, including *Dibamus ingeri*

Family Xenosauridae: 2 genera, 6 species of knob-scaled lizards and crocodile lizards, including *Shinisaurus crocodilurus*

Family Anguidae: 12–14 genera, 113 species of alligator lizards, glass lizards, and slow worms, including southern alligator lizard, *Elgaria multicarinata*, and the slow worm, *Anguis fragilis*

Family Varanidae: 1 genus, about 57 species of monitor lizards, including Komodo dragon, *Varanus komodoensis*

Family Helodermatidae: 1 genus, 2 species of beaded lizards, including Gila monster, *Heloderma suspectum*, Mexican beaded lizard, *H. horridum*

Family Lanthanotidae: 1 species, Borneo earless monitor, *Lanthanotus borneensis*

Total: 20 families, about 418–429 genera, over 4,700 species

its name printed on this page. Several other geckos in the genus, all from West Indian islands, are only slightly longer. The tiny ground chameleon, *Brookesia minima,* and related stump-tailed *Brookesia* chameleons from Madagascar have a smaller overall length of 1.38 inches (3.5 cm), but because they have very short tails, their body length is slightly more than that of the dwarf gecko.

Legs and Locomotion

Lizards' shapes vary almost as much as their sizes. Typically they have four limbs, but they can be large and powerful, as in iguanas, or short and almost redundant. In normal locomotion the lizard moves one front leg and the opposite hind leg at the same time. Then the legs alternate, and the lizard goes along in a wriggling motion. In many species the hind legs are much longer than the front ones, and several run only on their hind legs when they get up speed. This is known as bipedal locomotion and is most common in agamids, iguanids, and monitors. The South American basilisk, *Basiliscus basiliscus*, has extended the technique to include running across the surface of water and is known locally as the "Jesus Christ lizard." A second species, *B. plumifrons*, is also able to run across the surface. Some lizards use their hind legs to support themselves as they stand up to survey their surroundings or confront their enemies.

Toes can be long and spindly or short and stumpy depending on their function: Long toes are useful in climbing, while short ones are associated with digging. The toes of some species, notably many geckos, have

⊖ *Geckos' toes have sophisticated modifications that help them climb and stick to smooth surfaces. Seen here is the foot of the tokay gecko,* Gekko gecko.

broad pads immediately behind the claws that enable them to climb smooth surfaces. A few species of geckos even have webs between the toes. In the case of the so-called flying geckos, *Ptychozoon kuhli* from Southeast Asia, the webs enable them to glide from tree to tree. In the Namibian web-footed gecko, *Palmatogecko rangei*,

"Look, No Legs!"

An evolutionary tendency for limbs to disappear altogether or to be reduced to the point where their function is dubious has happened independently in several unrelated lizard families. The snake lizards, Pygopodidae, have lost their front limbs completely, and their hind limbs are reduced to barely noticeable scaly flaps. All 15 species of the blind lizard family, Dibamidae, are completely legless. Other families, such as the whiptails and racerunners, Teiidae, the girdled lizards, Cordylidae, and the microteiids, Gymnophthalmidae, have some species with well-developed limbs and others with reduced or absent limbs.

Within the Scincidae there is a very strong tendency toward limb reduction. All members of the subfamily

Acontinae (with 18 species from southern Africa) lack limbs, as does the European limbless skink, *Ophiomorus punctatissimus*. Some Australian skinks in the genus *Lerista* have a pair of small hind legs and no front legs, and the genus *Chalcides* from the Mediterranean region shows the whole gradation from legged to legless skinks. Similarly, the alligator lizard family, the Anguidae, contains species with normal proportions as well as others with no limbs at all, such as the European slow worm, *Anguis fragilis*, the glass lizards, *Ophisaurus* from Europe and North America, and both species of the legless lizards, *Anniella* from California and Baja California.

Leglessness in a number of families seems to have evolved in response to a burrowing lifestyle and is a striking example of convergent evolution. Not all species are out-and-out burrowers, however—some live among thick vegetation where long limbs would be a hindrance. Species with small legs may use them when crawling slowly. However, when moving quickly or when burrowing, they lay them flat against their bodies.

The eastern glass lizard, Ophisaurus ventralis *from North America, is legless and could easily be mistaken for a snake. However, unlike snakes, it has movable eyelids and external ear openings.*

they act as snowshoes, allowing it to run swiftly over the loose, powdery sand on which it lives. Burrowing species tend to have small, reduced limbs. They move through loose sand by wriggling rapidly from side to side with their legs held against their bodies in a process known as "sand swimming." The lizard that is most adept at this is probably the North African sandfish, *Scincus scincus*.

Many lizards live in trees. Adaptations to an arboreal lifestyle may be slight, as in iguanids and agamids, whose long limbs and digits are equally useful in trees or on the ground. In extreme cases species are so well suited to climbing that they are almost helpless on the ground, for example, chameleons. Their digits are fused into two groups arranged opposite each other that act as pincers to grip branches and twigs. Their tails are prehensile to provide a fifth point of attachment, and their leaflike shape and legendary camouflage protect them against predators. Their elastic tongues enable them to mop up the insects that other lizards cannot reach. There are arboreal lizards in other families, including the geckos, anoles, and monitors, but none that are so wonderfully adapted to life high in the trees as the chameleons.

Scales

Lizards are covered in scales, but in no other group of reptiles is there so much variation in their size, shape, and arrangement. They can be large and overlapping or small, rounded, and close together (granular). Many species have a mixture of types. Sometimes, as in the chameleons, they have odd, studlike scales scattered throughout an otherwise uniform surface of small, granular scales. The scales of many species (for example, the girdle-tailed lizards, *Cordylus* species from Africa, and the alligator lizards, *Gerrhonotus* from North America) are thickened to form a kind of armor plating that protects them from drying out and from predators.

The scales of the Australian stump-tailed skink, *Trachydosaurus rugosus*, are among the largest and most knobby, making it look like a pine cone on legs. Other skinks have glossy, overlapping scales or heavily keeled scales arranged in rows. The Gila monster, *Heloderma suspectum*,

⬅ *The jagged scales of the Texas spiny lizard,* Sceloporus olivaceus, *resemble the sharp edges of tree bark. They aid in camouflage as well as defense.*

and the Mexican beaded lizard, *H. horridum*, have scales consisting of thick, circular beadlike studs arranged in regular rows and surrounded by thick skin. Many species, including the wall lizards, Lacertidae, and the night lizards, Xantusidae, have large, rectangular belly scales arranged in transverse rows.

Lizards of some families have small, platelike bones called osteoderms lying just below the surface. Notable examples are the skinks, Scincidae, the slow worm and alligator lizard family, Anguidae, and the African plated lizards, Gerrhosauridae.

Decorative Features

Many iguanids, chameleons, and agamids have flaps, frills, crests, or other ornamentation made up of (or covered by) scales. They are often larger and more prominent in males, and include the row of long, toothlike scales running down the center of the lizard's back and tail in iguanas and others. There are also the spiky scales found on the heads of some Asian agamas and on the necks and flanks of the American horned lizards, *Phrynosoma*. Other agamas from South Asia have horns on their snouts; but the most highly decorated horned lizards are the chameleons, especially Jackson's chameleon, *Chamaeleo jacksonii* from East Africa, in which the male has three long, tapering horns projecting from its head, resembling the prehistoric *Triceratops*.

The function of these accessories is often connected with display and communication to other members of the same species, but they also have a disruptive purpose, breaking up the lizard's outline when it is at rest and helping it avoid the attention of predators. Flaps and frills in species such as the leaf-tailed geckos, *Uroplatus* from Madagascar, and *Phyllurus* from Australia, have the same function. They act as a "cloak" to smooth out the lizard's shape and eliminate shadows.

The Senses

Many lizards rely heavily on sight to capture prey, avoid predators, and interact with their own species. However, as in many animals, they are better at detecting moving objects than stationary ones. Special types of eyes are found in several groups. Burrowing species often have only rudimentary eyes, sometimes covered with skin, as in the blind lizards, Dibamidae. Geckos, snake lizards, and night lizards do not have movable eyelids. Instead, as in snakes, the eyes are covered by a transparent scale (the brille) that owes its origins to fused upper and lower eyelids. Their eyes are therefore "closed" all the time, and the lizards see out of a window in the eyelid. They keep the brille clear of dirt and dust by licking it constantly with their tongue, and it is shed with the rest of the skin. In a few other species the eyelids are movable, but the lower one still has a transparent window. It probably protects the eye from windblown sand and dust and when the lizard is burrowing.

Nocturnal lizards, especially the geckos, have large eyes, sometimes with brightly colored irises. Like cats, they have vertical pupils that can be closed down to narrow slits in response to bright light, with just a few "pinholes" to see through. Chameleons have remarkable eyes. Each eyeball is surrounded by a turret of skin formed from the fused upper and lower eyelid, with just a small circular opening. By rotating the turret, the chameleon can look in any direction; and since the turrets move independently of each other, it can actually look in

⊖ *The huge eyes with their brown-red irises and vertical pupils hint at the nocturnal habits of Palmatogecko rangei, the web-footed gecko from Namibia.*

seconds and carries for hundreds of yards across the gravelly or sandy plains.

Food and Feeding

Between them the lizards eat a wide variety of food. Some species will eat more or less anything, while others are highly specialized. Examples of specialists include the thorny devil, *Moloch horridus*, which eats only ants; Burton's snake lizard, *Lialis burtoni*, which eats only other lizards; and the marine iguana, *Amblyrhynchus cristatus*, which lives exclusively on seaweed.

The majority of lizards are carnivorous, and the most common prey is insects and other invertebrates. They are abundant and of a size that is easily dealt with by most small- to medium-sized lizards. Larger prey, such as small vertebrates (including other reptiles and mammals), is only available to the larger, more powerful kinds, notably monitor lizards and the beaded lizards.

As a rule, hunting methods are unsophisticated: The lizard sees the prey, chases and catches it, and chews until it can swallow it. Many species rely on ambush tactics, but others search actively for prey. Most lizards probably use an intermediate strategy—they wait in one place, often basking; if they see prey within striking distance, they go after it, returning to their basking spot once the chase is over. Chameleons, of course, are unusual—they use their protrusible tongue to "zap" insect prey from a distance that can be greater than their own body length.

Enemies and Defense

Lizards have many enemies, not least other lizards. Defensive strategies have evolved along several lines. The first line of defense is to avoid being noticed. If noticed, the next best thing is not to be caught or to look as unappetizing as possible. As a result, many lizards are well camouflaged to match the surfaces on which they usually live (known as cryptic coloration): Sand dwellers are pale yellow; leaf dwellers are green; bark dwellers are

⊕ *Like many lizards,* Lacerta vivipara, *the common or viviparous lizard from Europe, feeds mainly on invertebrates. This one is devouring a large cranefly.*

two directions at the same time. When hunting, it can use one eye to look over its shoulder for predators while the other fixes on the prey.

Members of most lizard families have openings to their eardrums, but in some species they are covered with scales. Chameleons, however, are stone deaf. They have no ear opening and no middle-ear cavity. It is difficult to assess how important the sense of hearing is to lizards, but in geckos and snake lizards sound is a means of communication. Many of these species are nocturnal, and they use a variety of barks, grunts, and squeaks to keep in touch with each other. In fact, "gecko" is an alliteration of the sound made by some Asian species, as is "tokay," one of the more common species. Male barking geckos, *Ptenopus* species from southern Africa, call to each other from the entrances to their burrows with a loud, characteristic sound that lasts for several gray, and so on. Plain camouflage is not common, however, and most cryptically colored lizards also have textures that match the surface. Foremost among them are the leaf-tailed geckos of Madagascar, *Uroplatus* species, and Australia, *Phyllurus* species, which can be impossible to see when they sit still on lichen-covered tree trunks. Chameleons come a close second in the camouflage stakes, but there are many more examples.

Many cryptic species sit very still even when approached, but most lizards run away when they sense they have been spotted. They may retreat into a burrow or into crevices in rocks or trees. Some species, such as the African flat lizards, *Platysaurus* species, can slip into narrow cracks. Others, such as the American chuckwallas, *Sauromalus* species, inflate their bodies to jam themselves in. Basilisks, *Basiliscus* species, are famous for their ability to run across the surface of water, and several other lizards, notably the green iguana, *Iguana iguana*, and the Chinese crocodile lizard, *Shinisaurus crocodilurus*, dive underwater to escape capture. A few lizards, such as the Asian flying geckos, *Ptychozoon kuhli*, and flying lizards, *Draco volans*, even take to the air, leaping from high branches and gliding down to safety.

As a last resort, lizards defend themselves by biting, bashing, or scratching their enemy. Many have long teeth and powerful jaws—a bite from a monitor, agama, or a tokay gecko can leave a surprised human bleeding. Only two species, the Gila monster, *Heloderma suspectum*, and the Mexican beaded lizard, *H. horridum*, are venomous. They have grooved teeth in their lower jaws along which venom flows (unlike venomous snakes that deliver venom through fangs in their upper jaws).

Some lizards are good bluffers, squaring up to their aggressor and even jumping at it with an open mouth.

In Australia the central bearded dragon, *Pogona vitticeps*, and the frilled lizard, *Chlamydosaurus kingii*, raise their large beards or frills to intimidate their enemies. American horned lizards, *Phrynosoma* species, may squirt blood from their eyes, and juvenile bushveld lizards, *Heliobolus lugubris,* mimic beetles that squirt a noxious substance into the face of predators. Other examples of mimicry include some Australian snake lizards that resemble venomous snakes and a small gecko, *Teratolepis fasciata* from the Middle East, whose tail is supposedly shaped like the head of a viper.

Discarded Tails

Lizards from a number of families can discard part of their tail when under severe threat. The strategy, known as caudal autotomy, is especially well developed in the geckos, skinks, wall lizards, racerunners, whiptails, and the glass lizards, and is found in several other families. In fact, there are only five families in which caudal autotomy does not happen. The breakage occurs across a fracture plane found on several vertebrae in the lizard's tail. Associated with the fracture plain are bundles of muscles that cause the tail to come away from the rest of the lizard's body and to continue wriggling. While the muscles twitch, the tail holds the predator's attention, and the rest of the lizard can slip away. A replacement tail begins to grow immediately, but the new one will look different from the original. There is no limit to the number of times a regrown tail can autotomize. In some skinks the tail is brightly colored; as a result, predators are encouraged to attack the tail rather than the lizard's head or body.

← **Uroplatus fimbriatus,** *the leaf-tailed gecko, avoids detection by using camouflage colors that blend in with tree bark, moss, and lichens found in its native Madagascan habitat.*

→ *If its camouflage colors fail to hide it from an enemy, the leaf-tailed gecko,* Uroplatus fimbriatus, *creates a startling warning display by opening its mouth wide to reveal a bright red tongue.*

Agamas and Dragon Lizards

The family Agamidae contains about 430 species of agamas and dragon lizards in 49 genera. They occur only in the Old World and are especially common in Australia, Asia, the Middle East, and throughout Africa. One species, *Laudakia stellio*, ventures into southeastern Europe, but they are absent from Madagascar. Common names vary from place to place, but "dragon lizards" is often used (mainly in Australia), while "agamas" is the term used in Africa. Chisel-toothed lizards is a general term used to describe the main feature that distinguishes them from the iguanids, which they otherwise resemble in many ways.

The teeth in question are firmly attached to the top edges of the upper and lower jawbones (and known as acrodont), whereas those of iguanids and most other lizards are less firmly attached and are joined to the sloping inside edges of the jawbones (known as pleurodont). Agamid teeth are often fused together to form broader, chisel-shaped teeth more like those of mammals than the typical pointed teeth of most lizards.

Agamids live in a variety of habitats from dense tropical forests to some of the world's most arid places, for example, in the central desert of Australia and in parts of the Sahara and the Namib Deserts. Although there are fewer agamid species than iguanids, they are equally varied in shape, color, and ornamentation, and they have adapted to an equally wide range of situations. One group of agamas, the flying dragons, has mastered an element that iguanids never have. Unlike the iguanids, the agamids have not been subdivided into subfamilies.

Characteristics

Although there is no such thing as a "typical" agamid, they do have certain features in common. All agamids have four functional legs. They often have broad, triangular heads (when seen from above) and long tails with round cross-sections. Many species have plump, almost pear-shaped bodies, although a number are more slender. They have large eyes, good vision, and many are very colorful. There is often obvious sexual dimorphism,

---

Common name Agamas and dragon lizards **Family** Agamidae

Family Agamidae 49 genera, about 430 species of agamas, dragon lizards, or chisel-toothed lizards, including:

Genus *Acanthocerus*—20 species of tree and rock agamas from Africa, the Middle East, and Asia

Genus *Acanthosaura*—8 species of prickly lizards from Southeast Asia, including the pricklenape lizard, *A. crucigera*

Genus *Agama*—31 species of agamas from Africa and the Near East, including the red-headed rock agama, *A. agama*

Genus *Bronchocela*—7 bright green species of forest dragons from Southeast Asia

Genus *Calotes*—21 species of garden lizards from Southeast Asia, including the garden lizard, or bloodsucker, *C. versicolor*

Genus *Ceratophora*—5 species of horned agamas from Sri Lanka

Genus *Chlamydosaurus*—1 species of frilled lizard from Australia and New Guinea, *C. kingii*

Genus *Ctenophorus*—21 species of dragon lizards from Australia

Genus *Diporiphora*—13 species from Australia

Genus *Draco*—28 species of flying lizards from Southeast Asia, including the common flying lizard, *D. volans*

Genus *Hydrosaurus*—3 species of sail-fin lizards from Southeast Asia, including the Philippine sail-fin lizard, *H. pustulatus*

Genus *Hypsilurus*—13 species of forest dragons and angle-headed lizards from Australia and the South Pacific, including Boyd's forest dragon, *H. boydii*

Genus *Moloch*—1 species of thorny devil from Australia, *M. horridus*

Genus *Laudakia*—20 species of whorl-tailed agamas from southeast Europe and the Middle East, including the hardun, *L. stellio*

Genus *Leiolepis*—7 species of butterfly lizards from China and Southeast Asia, including the common butterfly lizard, *L. belliana*

Genus *Phrynocephalus*—43 species of toad-headed agamas from Central Asia and the Middle East

Genus *Physignathus*—2 species of water dragons from Australia and Southeast Asia

Genus *Pogona*—8 species of bearded dragons from Australia, including the central bearded dragon, *P. vitticeps*

Genus *Tympanocryptis*—8 species from Australia

Genus *Uromastyx*—16 species of dab lizards, or mastigures, from North Africa and the Middle East, including the spiny-tailed dab lizard, *U. acanthinurus*

SEE ALSO Lizards **44**:24; Agama, Red-Headed Rock **44**:38; Lizard, Spiny-Tailed Dab **44**:52; Iguanas **44**:80

The green tree agama, or green crested lizard, Bronchocela cristatella, is a large, arboreal lizard that inhabits forests in Southeast Asia and can also be found in disturbed areas and parklands.

The large tree agama, Acanthocerus atricollis, lives on tree trunks, rocks, and walls, where it hunts for ants and other arthropods. Males of the species are characterized by a bluish head as seen here.

with males being brightly colored while females and juveniles of the same species are dull and camouflaged. Males often have elaborate crests and frills, which may also be present to a lesser extent in females. The scales of many species are fairly large but uniform in size, and they often end in points or spines. Other species, however, have smaller scales and a silky texture to their skin.

They are all predominantly diurnal, and they live on the ground or in trees, although many use burrows as shelters into which they retreat at night or during very hot or very cold weather. A few live along watercourses and will take to the water if necessary to escape from predators. The flying lizards take to the air for the same reason. All species are carnivorous with the exception of the dab lizards, or mastigures, *Uromastyx* species, which are herbivores; some of the carnivorous species also take plant material occasionally.

All the agamids for which information exists are egg layers, but it has been suggested that one or more of the toad-headed agamas, *Phrynocephalus* species from

Central Asia, bear live young—several have body shapes that are similar to those of live-bearing iguanids such as the horned lizards, *Phrynosoma*.

There are many parallels between species or groups of species within the Agamidae and the Iguanidae, including the American horned lizards, *Phrynosoma* species, which parallel the Australian thorny devil, *Moloch horridus*; the American chuckwallas, *Sauromalus obesus*, which are similar to the Middle Eastern and North African dab lizards; and the Central American basilisks, *Basilicus* species, which share features with the water dragons and sail-fin lizards, *Physignathus* and *Hydrosaurus* species from Southeast Asia and Australia.

Origins and Relationships

The agama family is widely believed to have originated in Australia, where it remains one of the predominant lizard families. Fossils belonging to the genus *Physignathus* (water dragons) have been found in Early Miocene deposits, making them about 20 million years old. However, *Physignathus* is probably not closely related to other Australian agamids, but it has a close relative in Asia. Scientists think that the early agamids first appeared in Australia more than 20 million years ago. Some spread north into Asia and evolved into different forms, including *Physignathus*, which then moved back to Australia.

One species, *Physignathus lesueurii*, is the present-day representative of the genus in Australia, while *P. cocincinus* remained in Southeast Asia. The water dragon is restricted in Australia to the temperate northeastern forests, as is another agamid genus, *Hypsilurus*, the angle-headed lizards. There are two species in Australia and 11 in New Guinea and Indonesia. Angle-headed lizards have angular heads with crests and dewlaps fringed with large, toothlike scales.

All three of the forest-dwelling Australian agamids (*Physignathus lesueurii, Hypsilurus boydii*, and *H. spinipes*) are clearly more like the agamas of the tropical forests of Southeast Asia. All the remaining Australian agamids, however, are more closely related to each other; scientists have given them the clumsy name of "amphiboluroids." Amphiboluroid agamas occupy every possible ecological niche in Australia from tropical forests to arid, blistering deserts and everything in between.

Diporiphora species are mostly terrestrial, but they climb into low bushes. Between them they have a distribution that covers most of Australia and extends into New Guinea. They tend to be more slender than many agamids, and several are marked with light-colored stripes running along their bodies. *Diporiphora superba* lives among acacia trees and spinifex clumps in the Kimberley region and is overall bright green.

The other large genus is *Ctenophorus*, whose members are characterized by small, uniform scales covering their bodies—some species also have a dorsal crest consisting of slightly larger scales. They are ground-dwelling lizards, often with intricate and cryptic coloration. However, the males may have brightly colored heads and necks during the breeding season.

The *Pogona* species are known as bearded dragons. They are terrestrial species that occasionally climb onto tree trunks and stumps. Some of the larger *Pogona* species can expand their neck region, which is covered with pointed scales, erecting the "beard" that gives them their common name.

Members of *Tympanocryptis* are called earless dragons owing to the absence of external ear openings. They are six small, ground-dwelling lizards with markings that match the surfaces on which they live. The remaining Australian agamids are in monospecific (single-species) genera and include the thorny devil, *Moloch horridus*, and the frilled lizard, *Chlamydosaurus kingii*.

Southeast Asian Species

Southeast Asia is home to numerous genera of agamids, most of which live in warm and humid rain forests. The genus *Calotes* contains about 20 species of beauty lizards, garden lizards, or bloodsuckers. They are typical dragons and are mostly arboreal. The common garden lizard, *C. versicolor*, has a wide range from Southeast Asia through the Indian subcontinent and across Central Asia to the Middle East. It also occurs on some Indian Ocean island groups, including Mauritius and the Maldives, where it has been introduced.

Garden lizards are common and can often be seen perching on vertical fence posts and buildings as well as tree trunks. Other species previously included in *Calotes* have been reclassified as *Pseudocalotes* and *Bronchocela*. Many species have brilliant-green coloration and live among the foliage of shrubs and secondary forests. They have low crests of large, pointed scales, and males are probably territorial, although none have been studied thoroughly. The mountain lizards, *Japalura*, of which there are 23 species from China and Southeast Asia, are equally attractive but also poorly known.

Many of the strangest agamids have cryptic shapes and colors, and are hard to find even when resting in full view. The Malaysian armored spiny dragon, *Acanthosaura armata*, and the similar *Gonocephalus chamaeleontinus* rarely move if they sense danger. Instead, they cling motionless to a branch or sapling, which makes them easy to overlook. Both species have long, prickly spines on the nape of the neck and over their eyes. The pricklenape lizard, *Acanthosaura crucigera* from the same part of the world, is similarly adorned and is sometimes seen in the pet trade. The three sail-fin lizards, *Hydrosaurus*, have high crests on their heads and backs and are associated with watercourses. They come from Indonesia and the Philippines, and are among the largest agamids. Farther north and west the habitat becomes drier, and agamids are very different. Most are smaller and stockier, often with a rounded body shape.

⊕ *The angle-headed lizard,* Hypsilurus dilophus *from New Guinea, shows the angular, crested head and fringed dewlaps typical of the genus.*

⊕ Hydrosaurus pustulatus, *the Philippine sail-fin lizard, is threatened throughout most of its range by habitat destruction and overhunting for food and the live animal trade.*

The toad-headed agamas, *Phrynocephalus*, live in the deserts and steppes of Central Asia, the Middle East, and the Arabian Peninsula, living on sand or gravel flats. There are about 40 species in total, all quite similar with flattened bodies, wide heads, and thin, spindly limbs. They retreat into burrows at night or if in danger.

One of the commonest species is *Phrynocephalus mystaceus* from southern Russia, the Caspian region, and into southern China. When threatened, it raises the front of its body by straightening its long front legs and gapes with its mouth. At the same time, it opens a flap at each side of its mouth to make itself look bigger. The flaps and the inside of its mouth turn bright red as the lizard hisses, swings its tail around rapidly, and jumps at its aggressor. Other species in the genus also have these flaps. Another species, *P. helioscopus*, holds its tail above its head, exposing its red underside, probably to signal to other members of its own species but possibly to act as a warning to predators. This species in particular is incredibly difficult to see against the clay and stony deserts in which it lives.

In the same general region (but in more rocky habitats, including mountain ranges) the predominant genus is *Laudakia*, the whorl-tailed agamas. Their name comes from the large scales arranged in rings on their tails. They used to belong to the genus *Agama*. There are 20 species altogether, one of which, *L. stellio*, the hardun, extends into Europe around the eastern shores of the Mediterranean and onto a few Greek islands.

"True" Agamas

The genus *Agama*, which gives the family its name, has been much reduced in size since several groups of species were moved into other genera. However, it still contains 31 species. They are all active, fast-moving lizards. The males are conspicuous because of their bright coloration and their habit of taking up elevated positions on rocks and trees. Most are African, but they extend into the Middle East.

Two genera of agamids, the butterfly lizards, *Leiolepis*, and the dab lizards, *Uromastyx*, are often placed in a separate subfamily, the Leiolepidinae. However, their relationship with each other and with the other agamids is unclear. There are seven species of butterfly lizards occurring in China and Southeast Asia. The flanks of several species are marked with red and black, and they can expand their ribs to a limited degree, thereby flattening their body and exposing their bright flanks

⤓ *Toad-headed agamas, such as* **Phrynocephalus mystaceus,** *live in dry desert habitats from the Middle East to Central Asia. Their toes are partially fringed to enable them to walk easily across sand.*

Sri Lankan Specialties

① **Lyriocephalus scutatus,** *the hump-nosed lizard, lives on the ground and in trees in the hill forests of Sri Lanka. It displays the deep red color of its mouth in a defensive posture.*

Some Sri Lankan agamids form a unique group. Of 13 species, 10 are endemic, and there are new species waiting to be described. Although the widespread genus *Calotes* is represented here with six species, including the ubiquitous garden lizard, *C. versicolor*, the most interesting species are from three endemic genera: the horned agamas, *Ceratophora*; the pygmy agama, *Cophotis ceylanica*; and the hump-nosed lizard, *Lyriocephalus scutatus*. These unusual lizards live in the few remaining patches of rain and cloud forests, especially in the Knuckles Range in the center of the island.

The hump-nosed lizard, as its name suggests, has a large, rounded swelling on its snout, and it also has a semicircular crest on its neck. It lives mainly in hill forests. The pygmy lizard is found in two separated habitats: the Knuckles Range and a small area of cloud forest farther south. Its population fell sharply a few years ago when warm, dry weather (perhaps a result of global warming) affected its habitat, and large numbers of dead pygmy agamas were found over a period of just a few days. It is too early to tell whether or not numbers are recovering.

There are five species of so-called horned agamids in the genus *Ceratophora*, but two of them lack horns. They are also rain-forest species, but several are now more commonly seen in secondary forests where the original rain forest has been cleared for planting with commercial trees, especially cardamom. The rarest species, listed as IUCN Vulnerable, is the leaf-nosed lizard, *C. tennentii*, which lives only in one small area, much of which has been put under cultivation. Two recently described species, *C. karu* and *C. erdeleni*, have a total distribution of less than 4 square miles (10 sq. km) in the Morningside Forest Reserve. Their ranges overlap, but more studies will be needed before it is known whether they interact or compete with each other.

(hence the name butterfly lizard). There are unconfirmed reports that they can even glide; but since they are not arboreal, that seems unlikely.

Two species of butterfly lizards, *L. guentherpetersi* and *L. triploida*, are parthenogenetic (meaning they are female-only species that produce eggs without mating). Butterfly lizards are eaten in Thailand as well as being collected for the pet trade.

The dab lizards, or mastigures (the origins of both common names are unclear) make up a single genus, *Uromastyx*, with 16 species. They are from North Africa, the Horn of Africa (Somalia, Ethiopia, and Eritrea), and the Middle East. Dab lizards live in deserts and dig long tunnels in which to escape from extremes of temperature and from predators.

Common name Red-headed rock agama (rainbow lizard)

Scientific name *Agama agama*

Family Agamidae

Suborder Sauria

Order Squamata

Size 12 in (30 cm); males larger than females

Key features Body stocky; limbs and tail long; head wide and triangular; dominant males strikingly colored with blue body and yellow, orange, or brick-red head and a white stripe down the center of their back; subordinate males are duller; females and juveniles brown with spots of white and black

Habits Diurnal; terrestrial but climbs vertical surfaces well

Breeding Females lay 5–10 eggs in loose soil; eggs hatch after 50–60 days

Diet Insects, including ants; some plant material

Habitat Rocky places in deserts, grasslands, and sparse woodlands; often seen on and around buildings

Distribution West, central, and East Africa

Status Very common

Similar species There are many other agamas; females are easily confused with each other; males are distinctive, but the Mwanza flat-headed agama, *A. mwanzae*, is similar; however, its head is pink rather than orange-red

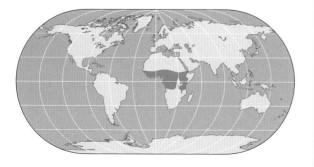

Red-Headed Rock Agama

Agama agama

Visitors to the East African game parks can hardly fail to notice the conspicuous, colorful red-headed lizards as they bask and display on rock outcrops and the walls of buildings.

A MALE RED-HEADED ROCK AGAMA in its prime is a spectacular lizard with electric-blue body and limbs and glowing orange head and neck. In the heat of the day the lizards bask on the most prominent rocks with their front legs outstretched and their body tilted toward the sun. At any hint of trouble—an approaching male, a female, or even a human observer—their color intensifies, and they bob their whole body up and down. This habit has not endeared them to the Moslem population of the region, which believes the lizards are mocking their movements during prayer.

Savage Fights

Encroaching males usually take the hint and move away; but if not, the bobbing becomes more rapid and exaggerated. The two lizards turn broadside to each other, head to tail, and begin to circle and sidestep, looking for a chance to attack. Eventually one of the males, usually the occupant of the territory, will rush the other, biting savagely with its fanglike teeth and using its tail as a whip or club.

A single attack is nearly always enough to send the intruder scurrying for cover, its color fading by the second. On rare occasions, however, maturing males get the better of established males, and there is a change in the hierarchy. One or two subordinate males—those whose colors are dull—are usually tolerated

⬆ *Not all red-headed rock agamas live up to their name. The colors of subordinate males are dull, while females and juveniles are brown with white and black spots.*

inside a territory, as are juveniles.
Females are also territorial, but their territories
are smaller, and several may be located within a
single male's territory. As a result, a social
structure of a single dominant male and a
harem of females develops. Because they are so
easily seen, interactions can be observed from a
distance as they unfold throughout the day.

Males mate with all the females that have
territories within their own. Mating probably
takes place throughout the warmer months of
the year, but egg laying is timed to coincide
with periods of heavy rain, usually during the
rainy season but sometimes during odd heavy
showers during the dry season. The rain is
essential to soften the otherwise baked soil and

allow the female to dig a
burrow. Rains also promote rapid plant growth
and in turn a proliferation of insects, which are
available by the time the hatchlings emerge.
Females find a patch of loose, moist soil often
in the shade of a tree, rock, or building in
which to lay their five to 10 eggs. Incubation
takes about 50 to 60 days, although nests are
often raided by predators, including
mongooses, before they hatch.

The young lizards measure about 3 to 4
inches (7.5–10 cm) in length and begin feeding
on small insects immediately. Activity patterns
of juveniles and adults are slightly different,

⊕ *The Mwanza
flat-headed agama,
Agama mwanzae, is
similar in appearance to
its relative the red-
headed rock agama, but
its head is pink instead
of orange.*

because small lizards warm up more quickly than large ones and are more active early in the day. They seem to find shelter either from the heat or from predators during the middle of the day. Juveniles are occasionally eaten by adults, and that may also affect their behavior. Adults remain active in the middle of the day except during the hottest months, when they retreat into cracks and crevices from late morning until

Agama Relatives

There are 31 species in the genus *Agama*. A further 20 species that were once included in *Agama* are now in the closely related genus *Acanthocerus*, the tree and rock agamas. The latter are larger, more thickset, and most of them live on vertical tree trunks. They tend to be less colorful than the *Agama* species, although males of some are marked with blue and green. Another 20 species have been placed in the genus *Laudakia* (they were also included in *Agama* previously). So about 70 species can broadly be referred to as "agamas."

Of the "true" agamas (those still in the genus *Agama*) many are colorful, active, and conspicuous lizards of roughly the same shape, size, and lifestyle. The Mwanza rock agama, *A. mwanzae*, replaces the red-headed rock agama in the Serengeti region and around the shores of Lake Victoria. It is, if anything, even more colorful, with a vibrant pink head, neck, shoulders, and chest, a bright blue lower back, tail, and limbs, and a pale blue line running down its back. Nondominant males and males that are not displaying lack the pink coloration but retain the blue areas. Females and juveniles are brown and similar to those of the red-headed rock agama. The Mwanza rock agama favors outcrops of rounded granite boulders, known locally as *kopjes,* or sheet rock with plenty of cracks. Like the red-headed rock agamas, they are sometimes found around game lodges and other buildings.

Farther south in South Africa the southern rock agama, *A. atra*, takes over. Males of this species are overall a darker color than the red-headed rock agama and have a bright blue head and a white or cream line running down their back. They are very common—almost every rock outcrop has a colony—and may occur at a density of up to 66 per acre (165 per ha). Their social structure is similar to that of the red-headed rock agama, with males having large territories and females having smaller ones. In Namibia the Namibian rock agama, *A. planiceps*, leads a similar life. This species has a red head, but it is a clear, coral red, not the same shade as that of *A. agama*. It is wary and even more difficult to approach than the red-headed rock agama.

⊖ *Other agamas are also territorial. Here* Agama aculeata, *the ground agama from South Africa, arches its back in a defensive pose.*

⊙ *With its extensive range and conspicuous, brightly colored males that perch on rocks and fence poles the southern rock agama,* A. atra, *is probably the most well-known lizard in South Africa.*

late afternoon. None of the agamas venture voluntarily onto the ground, preferring to remain on the rocks except when traveling from one outcrop to another or when laying eggs.

Enemies and Defense

Because they bask in exposed places, red-headed rock agamas (and other agamas) are exposed to predation, especially from aerial attack. They are, however, hard to approach, since they have good eyesight and keep a watchful eye open for predators, frequently swiveling their heads around to look up at the sky. Even at a distance of 100 yards (91 m) they will raise themselves up and do pushups if they sense approaching danger; but the way in which they react to a closer approach varies with temperature and other factors.

They are more likely to hold their ground when they are warmed up, presumably because they can react more quickly. When an intruder comes within 10 to 20 yards (9–18 m) they usually run away, but sometimes they flatten themselves to a rock, hoping to escape notice.

If they feel seriously threatened, agamas first try to outrun their enemy. They leap from rock to rock or run up sheer rock faces but will retreat into holes and crevices if necessary. They often reemerge after a few minutes and sometimes take up a basking position on the opposite side of the rock. Captured agamas can give a painful bite with their incisorlike teeth and can easily draw blood.

They have a wide variety of enemies, including birds such as various kestrels (*Falco* species), black-shouldered kites (*Elanus caeruleus*), and other birds of prey. Large males sometimes face up to small kestrels and kites, and drive them off, but smaller lizards have little defense other than to hide. Although it is difficult to quantify, snakes (especially nocturnal species such as spitting cobras, *Naja nigricollis* and *N. pallida*) probably take more agamas than any other predators. These snakes can seek them out and capture them at night while they are asleep; both species have been seen climbing the walls of buildings and catching sleeping agamas. Diurnal snakes, including sand snakes, *Psammophis* species, also take their fair share, as do small boys with stones.

Feeding

Agamas of all sizes are mainly insectivorous. They prefer ants, which they will take in large numbers by sitting next to a trail. They also catch flying insects, plucking them from the air by means of acrobatic leaps. Plant material, including leaves, flowers, and fruit is also eaten.

Common name Frilled lizard

Scientific name *Chlamydosaurus kingii*

Family Agamidae

Suborder Sauria

Order Squamata

Size From 24 in (61 cm) to 36 in (91 cm)

Key features A large lizard with a triangular head and a wide, circular frill around its neck; frill is normally folded along its neck and chest when at rest but raised when the lizard is alarmed; body usually brown; frill can range from brown to black, the latter having a red center

Habits Arboreal; diurnal

Breeding Egg layer with 8–14 eggs per clutch; eggs hatch after 54–92 days

Diet Insects and small vertebrates, including other lizards

Habitat Open woodland

Distribution North Australia and southern New Guinea

Status Common

Similar species None

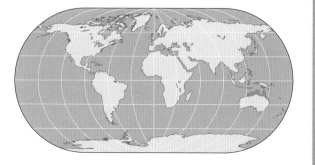

Frilled Lizard

Chlamydosaurus kingii

The frilled lizard is a spectacular dragon lizard from Australia. Its defensive display is unique in the reptile world.

WHEN AT REST, THE FRILLED LIZARD has a large flap of skin folded along the side of its upper body. When it feels threatened, it erects the flap to form an elaborate frill that completely encircles its head like a ruff. The frill is supported on long, slender bones radiating from the hyoid bones, which originate in the lizard's mouth and support the tongue. The extensions act like the struts of an umbrella. As the frill extends, the lizard opens its mouth widely to show the bright yellow interior; the wider it opens its mouth, the more the frill opens out. At the same time, it straightens its front limbs so that its head is held well off the ground. It can even stand up on its hind limbs to make itself look bigger than it really is.

The display may be reinforced by hissing and jumping at its enemy before turning and fleeing. It raises its front limbs off the ground as it goes, speeding along on its two long hind limbs until it reaches the safety of a tree. It is a good climber and clambers quickly out of reach. Frilled lizards also use their frills during encounters with individuals of the same species, and males may use them in territorial displays. Males also fight during the breeding season, biting and lashing each other with their tails.

Daily Activity

Their behavior pattern involves basking in the early morning by clinging vertically to a tree trunk and orienting their body to soak up as much heat as possible. Then during the hottest part of the day they move into the shade, often climbing higher into the crown of the tree where there is some breeze. They rarely venture out of the tree except in the early morning and late afternoon when, having spotted potential prey, they sprint across the ground to capture it before hurrying back to the safety of the tree.

SEE ALSO Agamas and Dragon Lizards **44:32**

⤓ Frilled lizards are famous for their dramatic defensive displays and have even been adopted as the reptile emblem of Australia. At rest, the frill acts as camouflage, allowing the lizard to blend in with the bark of a tree.

For such a large lizard the frilled lizard includes a surprising number of small prey such as ants and termites in its diet. This is simply because they are the most numerous prey species in the arid grassland and sparse woodlands in which it lives. Frilled lizards also eat larger invertebrates, small mammals, and other lizards when they get the chance.

They have very sharp eyes, and their hunting is done almost entirely by sight. Frilled lizards thrive immediately after the bush fires that sweep across their dry habitat with some regularity. Once the undergrowth of dead grasses has burned off, their prey is much easier to see from their elevated perches.

Frilled Lizard History

The frilled lizard was one of the first lizards to be described from Australia in 1825.

Its generic name, *Chlamydosaurus*, means "cloaked lizard," and its specific name, *kingii*, honors Rear Admiral Philip King, who commanded British naval ships that explored Australia in the 19th century. It is the only member of its genus.

Breeding takes place during the southern summer (November to April), which also coincides with the rainy season, when food is most abundant. Females lay eight to 14 eggs in a clutch, although numbers vary among populations living in different places, perhaps depending on food supply. Females typically bury their eggs in a patch of open sandy soil, where the nest will receive sunlight for most of the day.

Common name
Common flying lizard (flying dragon)

Scientific name *Draco volans*

Family Agamidae

Suborder Sauria

Order Squamata

Size From 6 in (15 cm) to 8 in (20 cm)

Key features Body slender with a long, thin tail and long, spindly legs; there is a flap of skin on each side of the body supported by elongated ribs; these "wings" are normally held against the side of the body but can be opened for gliding; wings are mottled orange and black; both sexes have a dewlap (piece of loose skin) on their throat that is yellow in males and blue in females

Habits Diurnal; arboreal, living on vertical tree trunks

Breeding Egg layer with clutches of 3–6 eggs buried in the ground

Diet Small insects, mainly ants and termites

Habitat Rain forests

Distribution Southeast Asia (Malaysian Peninsula, Indonesia, Borneo, and the Philippines)

Status Common

Similar species There are 28 species of flying lizard altogether, and their ranges overlap in many places; they are most easily distinguished by the color of their wings and dewlaps

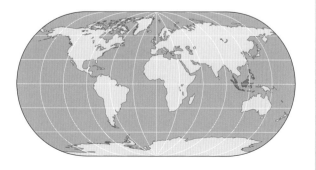

Common Flying Lizard

Draco volans

Flying lizards, of which Draco volans *is one of the most widespread species, live on large tree trunks in rain forests. They flit from one tree to another using their collapsible "wings."*

THE FLYING LIZARDS DO NOT ACTUALLY FLY—they glide between the trees. Their "wings" are formed from a membrane of skin supported by elongated ribs, usually five but sometimes six. The ribs are movable; and when the lizard is at rest, they fold down like an old-fashioned fan. During gliding, however, the first two ribs are swung forward by muscular contractions. They in turn pull the remaining ribs forward, because they are attached by ligaments. The wingspan is roughly equal to the lizard's body length.

Free-Falling

To glide, the lizard first drops from its resting place with its wings folded and its tail raised, so that it falls at a very steep angle. Almost immediately, however, it erects its wings and lowers its tail so that its rate of fall is slowed, and it glides almost horizontally. It uses its tail as a rudder to steer. Just before it lands, the lizard raises its tail again and changes the shape of its wings so that they scoop more air. These actions slow the lizard down and change its position so that its head is pointing up, in the same way as when an aircraft stalls. The lizard can then land lightly on its new tree trunk.

It runs up the tree immediately to regain the height lost during the glide. Flying lizards can glide for up to 50 yards (46 m), but their normal "flight" is much shorter, often a route between two neighboring tree trunks that are only a few yards apart. Taking the 28 species of the genus as a whole, small species can glide farther than large species; the common flying lizard, *D. volans*, is roughly intermediate in size.

↥ *The common flying dragon can glide considerable distances using lateral membranes stiffened by elongated ribs. It controls its descent with a degree of accuracy by small adjustments of the tail and membranes.*

Other Winged Reptiles

The only other flying lizards are the flying geckos, *Ptychozoon*, which also live in Southeast Asia, although there is evidence of limited gliding in another gecko, the wood slave, *Thecadactylus rapicauda* from Central and South America, as well as in a lacertid, the blue-tailed tree lizard, *Holaspis guentheri* from southern Africa. Flying snakes, *Chrysopelea*, are also found in Southeast Asia, as are a number of flying frogs, *Rhacophorus* species.

flying lizard, but females of all species have relatively larger wings. These probably enable them to fly even with the added burden of a clutch of eggs. In one species at least (*Draco melanopogon*) and possibly others, females have a larger head relative to body size than males. It might act as a counterweight to the eggs, which are carried in the abdomen. However, this theory begs the question of how the female lizard manages to allow for the larger head when she is not carrying eggs.

Flying lizards spend their entire lives high up in forest trees except during one activity: Females need to come down to the ground to lay their eggs. They are not agile on the forest floor and are very susceptible to predation. They lay small clutches of three to six eggs, which are elongated and spindle shaped with heavily calcified caps at each end. As far as is known, this type of egg is unique to flying lizards, but the reason for its shape is unknown. Details of incubation and the size and habits of the hatchlings are also unknown.

When at rest, the lizard holds its head away from the tree trunk, probably to give it room to raise and lower its dewlap. All flying lizards have dewlaps, but they vary in size, shape, and color according to species and sex. The common flying lizard has a triangular dewlap that is yellow in males and blue in females. The female's dewlap is smaller than the male's. Variations in color and shape of the dewlap help different species recognize one another, just as anole lizards in North, Central, and South America use their dewlaps.

Female *Draco volans* are slighter larger than males. That is not the case in every species of

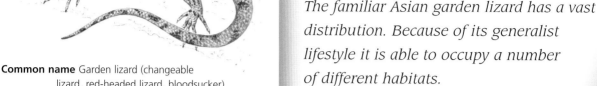

Common name Garden lizard (changeable lizard, red-headed lizard, bloodsucker)

Scientific name *Calotes versicolor*

Family Agamidae

Suborder Sauria

Order Squamata

Size To 20 in (51 cm)

Key features Body quite deep; limbs long, head triangular; snout pointed; there is a crest of enlarged scales on the nape of its neck; males are larger than females and have higher crests; light brown to buff in color with no markings on the body or with faint dark bands; males develop a red throat and chest during the breeding season

Habits Diurnal; mainly arboreal but sometimes ventures onto the ground

Breeding Egg layer; female may keep eggs in oviduct to lay later

Diet Insects and other invertebrates

Habitat Open forests, field edges, gardens, and parks

Distribution The Middle East (Iran and Afghanistan) through India and Sri Lanka, Indochina, South China, Hong Kong, and Sumatra; also several islands, including Andaman, Mauritius, and the Maldives (where it is probably introduced); also introduced to Oman

Status Very common

Similar species Other *Calotes* species and related genera are found throughout the region, but *C. versicolor* is by far the most common and the one most likely to be seen

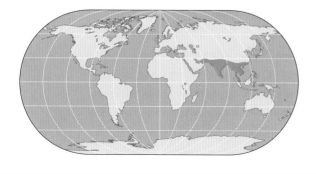

Garden Lizard

Calotes versicolor

The familiar Asian garden lizard has a vast distribution. Because of its generalist lifestyle it is able to occupy a number of different habitats.

IN CONTRAST TO SOME OTHER ASIAN AGAMIDS whose tiny ranges can be measured in hundreds of square yards, the garden lizard is found almost everywhere throughout the warmer parts of southern and Southeast Asia. It occurs from the Himalayan foothills to the steamy plains.

Blood-Red Throats

The garden lizard is a conspicuous diurnal species, often resting vertically on tree trunks and in bushes even near busy roads. It gets one of its common names, "bloodsucker," from the breeding coloration of the males. They take on a bright red flush to their heads, throats, and shoulders. They also develop jet-black patches on their neck and cheeks. At this time they are very aggressive toward each other, and their colors intensify or fade as they fight according to whether they are winning or losing—defeated males lose their bright colors and sulk.

Courting males raise their bodies as high as possible as they approach the female, who usually stays hidden. They extend a pouch in their throat (the "gular" pouch) while nodding their head slowly up and down. As they do so, they open and shut their mouth rapidly.

Because this species is so common, it has been studied quite thoroughly. Some of the results are very interesting, and they may apply to other lizards as well as the garden lizard.

Females have a very adaptable breeding cycle. At the beginning of the breeding season, which varies according to locality, females have good fat reserves. They use the stored energy to produce their first clutch of eggs. Subsequent clutches are produced from food eaten by the female at the time they are being formed. By

ⓣ **Calotes calotes, *the common green forest lizard from Sri Lanka and southern India, is a close relative of the garden lizard. It relies on its green coloration to protect it from predators.***

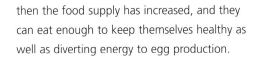

then the food supply has increased, and they can eat enough to keep themselves healthy as well as diverting energy to egg production.

Delayed Production

The ability to store energy is not their only trick. Females can store sperm in their oviducts for the whole breeding season if necessary. This allows them to lay more clutches without needing to mate again. What's more, females with eggs developing in their oviducts can put off laying them for up to six months if the conditions are not right, for example, if the weather turns cold and wet. Some scientists believe that egg retention in the oviduct may be a stepping stone toward viviparity (live birth) in lizards. There is a problem, however. If the eggs continued to grow in the oviduct, they would not be able to absorb enough oxygen to develop healthily, and the embryos would die. Furthermore, as the eggs absorbed moisture from the walls of the oviduct, they would continue to swell until they were too large to be laid. By reducing their body temperature to 73°F (23°C), females can arrest the development of their embryos.

Another adaptation is that both males and females only develop gametes (sperm or eggs) in the presence of the opposite sex. In experiments garden lizards were kept in isolation and in groups containing only the same sex. In both cases eggs and sperm failed to develop. In groups in which members of one sex had their testes or ovaries removed, sperm and eggs also failed to develop in the members of the opposite sex. This shows that they need to sense (probably through hormone release) that they are in a position to mate before expending energy on producing gametes.

Switching Genera

There are 21 species of *Calotes* altogether, but none are as widespread and adaptable as *C. versicolor*. A number of species that used to be included in the genus have been moved to another genus, *Bronchocela*. They are agile, bright green species that live in leafy shrubs. As in *Calotes*, the males have a low, serrated crest of pointed scales. *B. cristatella* is the most common species and is found throughout the Malaysian Peninsula and on Borneo. Its range in Singapore is thought to be declining because of competition with the garden lizard, which is better at adapting to man-made habitats.

Common name Thorny devil

Scientific name *Moloch horridus*

Family   Agamidae

Suborder   Sauria

Order   Squamata

Size   From 6 in (15 cm) to 7 in (18 cm)

Key features A weird-looking lizard; body squat, covered
                in large, thornlike spines; there is a very large
                spine over each eye, a raised, spiny hump on
                its neck, and 2 rows of spines along the top
                of its tail; dark reddish brown in color with
                wavy-edged, light tan stripes running over its
                head and down its body

Habits   Diurnal; terrestrial; slow moving

Breeding   Egg layer with a single clutch of 3–10 eggs;
                eggs hatch after 90–132 days

Diet   Ants

Habitat   Deserts

Distribution Western and central Australia

Status   Probably common in suitable habitat but
                rarely seen

Similar species There is nothing remotely similar in the
                region

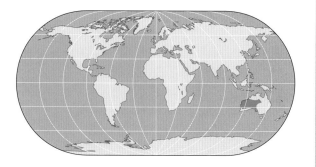

Thorny Devil

Moloch horridus

The thorny devil is Australia's answer to the American horned lizards, Phrynosoma, *with similar looks and lifestyle. Like the horned lizards, it is a dedicated ant-eater.*

THORNY DEVILS EAT NOTHING BUT ANTS, especially the very small species *Iridomyrmex flavipes* and others in the same genus. They lick them up at an estimated rate of 25 to 45 per minute. Their fecal pellets are round, glassy, and black. Unusually among lizards, each thorny devil uses its own individual place to deposit them, returning several days in a row until a small pile of distinctive droppings has accumulated.

Eating ants has its drawbacks: Many thorny devils are parasitized by nematodes (roundworms) that probably use the ants as an intermediate host.

Water Supplies

Drinking water is almost impossible to find in many of the dry, sandy places where thorny devils live, so the lizards have evolved an interesting system for capturing the dew that condenses on their body. A network of small channels covering their skin directs water by capillary action to the corners of the lizard's mouth. By gulping the water as it accumulates there, it can drink enough to compensate for the meager water content of its diet.

Thorny devils tolerate extremes of heat just as horned lizards do and remain feeding out in the open when other lizards have retreated into the shade. They have an average body temperature of 91°F (33°C). Even so, they are inactive during the hottest months of the year (January and February) and dig burrows into which they retreat to avoid the heat. They do not move around much in the coolest months (June and July) because they are too cold.

The lizards' activity patterns are easily studied by observing the distinctive tracks they make in their sandy habitat. In the summer they

⬇ **Moloch horridus** *is an extraordinary lizard that inhabits the dry Australian interior. It is covered in warty, thornlike spines, and narrow channels between its scales draw precious droplets of dew or rain into its mouth.*

Desert Lookalikes

range less than 10 yards (9 m) from their burrows; within this "home range" there will be one or more ant trails, a few small bushes with a pile of dead leaves or a loose tussock of grass beneath them, and a defecation site.

The thorny devils spend each night and the hottest part of each day in a burrow under one of the shrubs. Each day they venture a short distance from their refuge to feed, defecate, and eat some ants. In the spring, however, they are much more active, and trails across the sand often extend for more than 100 yards (91 m). These more adventurous trips are probably the result of an urge to mate. Studies have shown

There are many good examples of convergent evolution among lizards, but the pairing of the Australian thorny devil, *Moloch horridus*, with the American horned lizards, *Phrynosoma* species, is one of the best. The horned lizards belong to the Iguanidae, so they are only distantly related to the thorny devil. Both are food specialists, feasting on large numbers of ants. (The thorny devil eats nothing else.) Both live out in the open and use cryptic (disguise) coloring to avoid detection by predators. And both are well endowed with spiny scales.

Apart from the novelty value of finding similar animals on opposite sides of the world, the similarities tell us something about the way in which evolution works. Each evolutionary line is constantly "fine tuning" itself in response to the prevailing conditions. In time, evolution often comes up with similar solutions to similar problems regardless of which part of the world is involved.

that thorny devils home in on places where other members of their own species are, but nobody knows how they do it.

Spring Activity

The period of greatest activity is the southern spring and early summer (August to December), when mating and egg laying take place. Females lay a single clutch of three to 10 eggs each year. (They differ in this respect from the American horned lizards, which lay much larger clutches.) Females dig their nest tunnels on south-facing sides of sandy ridges, presumably because they are not subject to such extremes of temperature. The burrows have a right-angled bend in them, and the eggs are laid at the end in a chamber large enough to contain the clutch and a significant amount of air.

The female takes several days to dig the burrow. The temperature in the end chamber is a steady 88°F (31°C), and the eggs hatch after 90 to 132 days. The American herpetologist Professor Eric Pianka discovered that after the young had hatched and emerged from their nest, there were no traces of eggshells in the empty chamber. He concluded that the hatchlings had eaten them. If so, this is the only known case of reptiles eating their eggshells. The hatchlings are smaller versions of the adults, thorns and all.

49

Common name Central bearded dragon

Scientific name *Pogona vitticeps*

Family Agamidae

Suborder Sauria

Order Squamata

Size From 12 in (30 cm) to 16 in (41 cm)

Key features A thickset lizard with a slightly flattened body; back and neck covered with large spiny scales interspersed with smaller ones, a row of large conical scales runs around the edges of the back where it meets the underside; usually light brown in color but can also be yellowish brown or reddish brown; it has faint crossbands down the back and tail and stripes on its head that fade with age; throat is darker than the body, sometimes black

Habits Diurnal; terrestrial

Breeding Egg layer with large clutches of up to 35 eggs; eggs hatch after about 60 days

Diet Insects and plant material, especially flowers

Habitat Arid deserts and dry woodlands

Distribution Central Australia

Status Common

Similar species The eastern bearded dragon, *P. barbata*, lacks the row of conical scales along its flanks

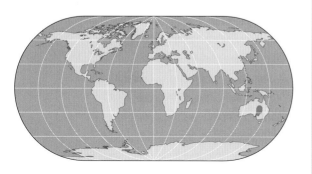

Central Bearded Dragon

Pogona vitticeps

The bearded dragon is a familiar sight in the central Australian desert, where it stations itself on top of fence posts, the stumps of dead trees, and small mounds of dirt at the roadside.

ALTHOUGH IT IS MAINLY TERRESTRIAL, the central beared dragon likes to bask in a prominent position and watch for predators and prey. Predators, especially snakes, are met with a spectacular display in which the lizard flattens its body, tilts it toward the danger, and lowers its beard. At the same time, it opens its mouth wide, showing off the bright yellow interior, and hisses.

Bearded dragons are very territorial, and both males and females will defend territories against newcomers. Males nod their heads and wave one of their forelimbs vigorously. Submissive males lower their bodies and heads until they are touching the ground, and wave their forelimbs slowly. This display pacifies the dominant male. If the newcomer does not submit, however, the male becomes very aggressive, especially in the breeding season, and the two lizards circle each other head to tail and attempt to bite the base of their rival's tail.

They accompany the routine by inflating their body, hissing, and lowering the skin on the beard. Eventually one of the males, usually the newcomer, runs away. Females also display by waving their forelimbs. A group of lizards made up of a dominant male, one or more submissive males, and several females soon establishes a hierarchy in which dominant animals feed first, and subordinate ones wait their turn.

Mixed Diet

Bearded dragons take a wide range of food, including small vertebrates, crickets, grasshoppers, and plant material, especially yellow flowers such as dandelions. They hunt

mainly by sight and have good vision, but they often use their tongue to investigate objects they have not experienced before. Young animals are more insectivorous than adults.

Being docile and apparently "intelligent," bearded dragons make good pets. They learn quickly to associate their owner with food. They breed well in captivity as long as a compatible pair or group is maintained, and the young grow quickly. They are also prolific—females lay about 20 eggs up to a maximum of 35. When incubated at 90°F (32°C), they hatch after about 60 days. A female in good health and with plenty of food and supplements can lay a clutch every three weeks throughout the summer.

All seven species of *Pogona* are called bearded dragons, and all have the ability to erect a beard, although some have more specialized skulls than others. *Pogona vitticeps* and *P. barbata*, whose specific name means "bearded," are the most accomplished.

⊖ *In an impressive display the central bearded dragon inflates its beard, which turns jet black. At the same time, it gapes to appear more intimidating.*

The Structure of the Beard

The bearded dragon raises its beard by means of modified bones on the floor of its mouth. The elongated bones are attached to the back of the hyoid bone, which is positioned within the lizard's tongue. To erect the beard, the lizard moves the whole apparatus forward until the hyoid bone can go no farther. Continued muscle contractions then force the back of the hyoid bone to tilt downward, which in turn causes the long bones to swing down and outward, taking the loose skin of the throat with it and making the pointed scales stand out.

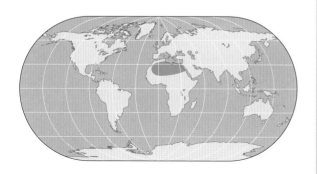

Common name
Spiny-tailed dab lizard

Scientific name *Uromastyx acanthinurus*

Family   Agamidae (sometimes placed in the subfamily Leiolepidinae)

Suborder   Sauria

Order   Squamata

Size   16 in (41 cm)

Key features A massive, thickset lizard with a broad body slightly flattened from top to bottom; head short (rather like a tortoise's); tail very large, armored with whorls of short, sharp spines and accounting for about one-third of the total length; color highly variable—juveniles are grayish brown, but adults can be brown, orange, brick-red, yellow, or green with black dots and squiggles; colors are brightest when the lizard is warmed up

Habits   Diurnal; terrestrial; retreats into burrows at night; lives in colonies

Breeding   Female lays clutches of up to 23 eggs in a burrow; eggs hatch after about 60 days

Diet   Plant material, especially flower buds, the soft tips of branches, and leaves

Habitat   Rocky slopes in valleys with seasonal water and thick, scrubby vegetation

Distribution North Africa (small mountain ranges within and surrounding the Sahara Desert)

Status   Common and widespread

Similar species Could only be confused with other *Uromastyx* species, of which there are about 16; *U. geyri,* which may be a subspecies of *U. acanthinurus*, is the only one whose range overlaps that of *U. acanthinurus*

Spiny-Tailed Dab Lizard

Uromastyx acanthinurus

Dab lizards live in underground burrows in some of the most arid, inhospitable landscapes of Africa and the Middle East. The spiny-tailed dab lizard is one of the most widespread and impressive species.

DAB LIZARDS LIVE IN COLONIES, like the chuckwallas, *Sauromalus* species (family Iguanidae) from North America, which they also resemble in appearance and in certain aspects of their behavior. Colonies are situated either in small valleys or gulleys with seasonal rivers that are dry most of the time, where dry riverbeds meet gravel plateaus, or at the edges of shallow basins that fill with water after rain. They also live near oases and in patches of hard ground between sand dunes (but never on loose sand). Only these conditions encourage growth of the tough, woody shrubs on which they feed.

Living in Colonies
Each colony has a system of burrows with oval entrances, the diameters of which depend on the size of the lizard living there. The burrows slope down at first before leveling out and are curved. Burrows can be up to 10 feet (3 m) in length with the main chamber 24 to 48 inches (61 cm–1.2 m) below the ground. In very rocky places the lizards excavate burrows under boulders or in cracks between them. Each adult has a main burrow and several subsidiary ones. Females' burrows sometimes have side chambers where they lay their eggs.

Population density depends largely on the amount of vegetation the habitat can support. In the most arid regions there may be just one dab lizard for every 20 acres (8 ha), but in places with relatively more lush vegetation there can be five to 10 lizards in each acre (0.4 ha). Even in a small area densities are highest on slopes with mixed vegetation and lowest on the rocky flats where fewer plants grow.

⊕ **Uromastyx acanthinurus** *is a medium-sized lizard. Its well-armored, spiny tail helps protect it from predators.*

Each colony has a home range centered on its burrows, measuring up to 2 acres (0.8 ha) in area. After winter rains thousands of annual plant seeds germinate quickly and produce a thick carpet of plants on which the lizards browse enthusiastically. Annual plants tend not to contain the toxins found in perennials, so they are easily digested and very nourishing. Once the annuals have withered and died, however, the lizards switch to eating the shrubs that grow in the dried-up riverbeds and may have to travel some distance to reach them—up to a mile (1.6 km) a day in some cases.

Temperature Preferences

The activity patterns of dab lizards are probably geared to barometric pressure. During rain storms and sand storms they stay in their burrows. During cool, overcast weather they emerge but do not venture far from the burrow entrances. On bright, sunny days they travel greater distances. They track from shrub to shrub, leaving distinctive trails as they drag their tails behind them. They rarely follow direct routes; instead, they take a winding course in order to avoid the burrows of other dab lizards.

They can withstand very high temperatures, but during extremely hot weather they may retreat during the middle of the day and become active at dusk. Their preferred temperature is around 100°F (38°C), and they bask with a flattened body until they reach it. Once they have achieved the right temperature, they change shape to expose as little of their body to the sun as possible. At higher temperatures they lift their body clear of the surface and pant. Panting, however, causes the lizards to lose moisture in the form of water vapor, and so they usually seek the shade of a rock or bush, or retreat back into their burrow

⊕ *Uromastyx ornata from North Africa is among the most spectacularly colored lizards in the genus. Males obtain their vivid green, blue, or yellow colors when they reach maturity at two or three years of age.*

if the temperature rises above 105°F (40°C). The surface of exposed rocks in the areas where they live can sometimes reach 161°F (72°C)!

Over most of their range winters can be cold, and the lizards hibernate. The length of hibernation depends on local conditions and can be from under a month to five or six months. They hibernate at a temperature between 57 and 85°F (14–22°C), which they can maintain for several months, living off fat stored in their thick tail. However, hot, dry conditions put a burden on their food reserves, and after several weeks their tails and limbs become emaciated. The lizards can tolerate conditions that are extreme even for reptiles and would rapidly prove fatal for most, perhaps all, other vertebrates. The mortality rate among young dab lizards is high—only about 10 percent reach maturity at the age of four years.

⊖ ⊘ *The chuckwallas in North America parallel the spiny-tailed dab lizards. Top:* Sauromalus varius, *the San Esteban chuckwalla, is the largest species. Right: The spiny chuckwalla,* S. hispidus *from Baja California, is distinctive among chuckwallas in having a spiny tail.*

Relatives and Counterparts

There are up to 16 species in the genus *Uromastyx*, although some of them may actually be subspecies. They range in size from 6 to 30 inches (15–75 cm) and include several other colorful species (notably *U. ornata*) as well as others that are drab. Some, including the spiny-tailed dab lizard, are used as food by local people, and others are collected for the pet trade where that is allowed. They range from North Africa through the Middle East and Arabia to Pakistan and India.

In North America the chuckwallas, *Sauromalus*, are a very close counterpart, but they are iguanids. Not only are they also herbivorous, but they are roughly the same size, they live among rocks and boulders, and they form colonies. There are six species, two of which live in the American Southwest and in Baja California. Four occur on islands in the Gulf of California. The best-known species is *Sauromalus obesus* from the driest parts of California, Nevada, Utah, Arizona, Baja California, and Sonora. Like the dab lizards, they are famous for wedging themselves into rock crevices by inflating their bodies.

Social Behavior

Dab lizards almost invariably live in colonies, and individual isolated burrows are rare. Colonies consist of up to 20 lizards. Both males and females are territorial. They puff up their body during confrontations, open their mouth, and hiss and bite. Physical contact is common, and they can damage each other badly with their powerful jaws.

Courtship takes place in the spring, but the exact timing depends on local conditions and is highly stereotyped. The male often waits at the entrance to the female's burrow for her to appear. Once she appears, he holds his body high off the ground to initiate courtship, then darts toward her and tries to get a grip on her side, neck, or front leg. At this point the female may decide to call the whole thing off by disappearing back into her burrow. If not, she often twists around and tries to bite the male's flank or the base of his tail. She may also use her tail to thrash the male's head.

These maneuvers cause the pair to move around in a circle until they either separate or mate, and the sequence may be repeated many times in the course of a day. Copulation takes place when the male twists his tail under that of the female, so that their cloacae are next to each other. It lasts only two minutes. Females often have many injuries by the end of the breeding season due to the attentions of males. Clearly, they need to be aggressive in order to ward off unwanted advances and minimizie injuries, and their survival depends on it.

Females lay their eggs in a side branch of their burrow, and clutches number up to 23 eggs. They can lay two clutches each year depending on the conditions. Once the clutch is complete, the female covers the eggs with soil. They hatch after about two months but may take more or less time depending on temperature. They are hardy and can tolerate temperatures above 97°F (36°C), but they require high humidity, otherwise they would collapse.

Hatchlings appear at the end of the summer. They measure about 3 inches (7.5 cm) and are gray in color. At first they eat insects and grubs in addition to plant material, and they grow quickly.

Diet of Plants

Adults prefer to feed on annual plants, which they eat in preference to woody species. They are important in building up fat reserves that see the lizards through periods of drought. However, they are available only for a short period each year or not at all in some years when there is no rain. For the rest of the year they eat a variety of tough perennials.

Each dab lizard works its way around the plants within its home range, locating potential foodstuff by sight, then testing it with their tongue before eating it. Plants are not destroyed or badly damaged because the lizards eat only the growing tips of twigs, leaves, and flower buds. They are able to obtain nourishment from plants that are poisonous to mammals, but they refuse certain species. Seeds that accumulate in hollows in the ground and between dunes are also eaten—the lizards crush them with their powerful jaws. In harsh conditions, however, they are less choosy and will even eat woody twigs and bark. They also eat beetles when there are not enough plants, and they will even eat the droppings of gazelles and their own feces. They have been known to survive a whole year without feeding.

Enemies and Defense

Adult dab lizards have relatively few predators, but juveniles have many, including foxes, wild cats, monitor lizards, snakes, and birds of prey. To avoid predation, they select a vantage point on which to rest and bask; if a predator approaches, they head for their burrow. Once there, they inflate their body by taking in air and wedge themselves in, using their tail to block access. If the burrow is between rocks, they are impossible to dislodge even with a pickax. If they are caught, they use their tail as a club. (*Uromastyx* means "tail whip," and *acanthinurus* means "spiny tail.") The spines on the tail can easily draw blood from humans.

Chameleons

The classification of the 131 chameleonid species is not definitive, but here they are grouped into six genera. Chameleons are unusual in appearance. They have evolved a number of special features that are ideally suited to an arboreal life and that set them apart from other lizards. They are distributed throughout the continent of Africa. A few species are also found in Spain, Portugal, the Middle East, Sri Lanka, India, and on the Seychelles Islands and Madagascar. About 50 percent of all known species live on Madagascar, including the largest, Oustalet's chameleon, *Furcifer oustaleti*, at 27 inches (69 cm) long, and the smallest, the tiny ground chameleon, *Brookesia minima* and relatives, which measure as little as 1.38 inches (3.5 cm) in length.

Habitat Types

There is a natural division of the environmental conditions in which chameleons occur throughout their range— either cool and dry or warm and humid. In tropical regions some species occur at high altitudes and are therefore subjected to temperatures similar to those in more temperate areas. In Central Africa the Senegal chameleon, *Chamaeleo senegalensis,* lives in lowland forest habitat and needs a constantly warm, humid environment. The coarse chameleon, *C. rudis,* is also from central Africa but lives in higher montane forests, where it is cooler and a little drier.

Chameleons live in three different types of habitat: highland, lowland, or forest floor. Highland habitat occurs between 2,000 and 9,900 feet (600–3,000 m), usually on mountain slopes. While daytime temperatures are similar to those at lower altitudes, night temperatures are considerably lower, resulting in a heavy morning mist that creates some humidity. The humidity evaporates when the sun warms the mountain slopes. The high-casqued chameleon, *Chamaeleo hoehnelii*, lives at about 9,250 feet (2,800 m) on the slopes of Mount Kenya, where overnight temperatures drop to freezing. Such conditions would kill most chameleons, but *C. hoehnelii* falls to the ground into leaf litter that helps keep it warm. When the first rays of the sun strike the following morning, it warms up and climbs back into the branches.

Lowland habitat is considered to be between 1,500 and 2,000 feet (500–600 m). In most areas it is a tropical rain-forest environment. Rainfall and humidity are usually high. Temperatures are fairly constant with little seasonal variation. The graceful chameleon, *C. gracilis,* is a typically equatorial species that enjoys the high humidity and heat.

Some species are found at the same altitude but in tropical scrub. These areas have a temperature similar to lowland rain forest, but rainfall is not as plentiful and

---

Common name Chameleons **Family** Chamaeleonidae

Family Chamaeleonidae 6 genera and about 131 species:

Genus *Brookesia*—23 species of stump-tailed chameleons from Madagascar, including *B. stumpffi*

Genus *Rhampholeon*—8 species of leaf chameleons from West Africa, including the western pygmy chameleon, *R. spectrum*

Genus *Bradypodion*—21 species of live-bearing dwarf chameleons from South Africa, including *B. thamnobates* and *B. damaranum*

Genus *Calumma*—18 species of chameleons from the more humid areas of Madagascar, including Parson's chameleon, *C. parsonii*

Genus *Furcifer*—19 species of chameleons from the more arid regions of Madagascar (2 species on the Comoro Islands), including the panther chameleon, *F. pardalis*

Genus *Chamaeleo*—42 species from Africa, the Middle East, Sri Lanka, India, and southern Europe, including the Namaqua chameleon, *C. namaquensis*, the veiled chameleon, *C. calyptratus*, and Jackson's chameleon, *C. jacksonii*

↑ **Chameleons
have physical
adaptations for life in the
trees, including grasping feet and
a prehensile tail. Chamaeleo hoehnelii, the high-
casqued chameleon, inhabits the slopes of Mount Kenya in Africa.**

motionless. High humidity levels in these areas encourage moss to grow—it even grows on the skin of *Rhampholeon spectrum*, giving it the appearance of a dying leaf.

Physical Features

Most chameleons' bodies are compressed from side to side. This shape allows them to move through leaves and twigs and, viewed head-on or from above, aids concealment. The body can be flattened even more to provide a larger area for heat absorption or to fool an enemy into thinking the chameleon is larger than it is.

Like other reptiles, chameleons are covered in scales. The scales can be quite small, making the body appear smooth, or large and often tubercular, giving it a rough appearance. Scales that are all the same size are said to be homogeneous. Heterogeneous means that the scales are different sizes. Most chameleons have areas of both types on different parts of the body. The skin is sloughed (shed) periodically. Unlike in snakes, whose old skin is usually sloughed in one piece, chameleon skin cracks and dries between the scales before falling off in many pieces. The chameleon sometimes needs to help the process by scraping along branches to remove old skin, especially around the eyes, since it can impair the chameleon's vision and therefore its ability to feed.

Various physical adornments add to the unusual appearance of many chameleons. Some species have horns (anything from one to four) or other hornlike processes. The latter may not be as rigid as horns; but like horns, they are probably of some sexual significance, since they usually occur in males. *Furcifer bifidus* from Madagascar has two large rostral (nose) processes. Most species have a crest of spines or blunt tubercles along the

tends to be seasonal. However, morning dew brings moisture that is beneficial to the chameleons. Oustalet's chameleon, *Furcifer oustaleti*, is thought to collect dew in its high casque, from where it runs down into its mouth.

Primary or untouched forest floor is the natural habitat for *Brookesia* and *Rhampholeon* species from Madagascar and West Africa respectively. Temperature and rainfall levels on the forest floor are the same as in lowland forest. Naturally decomposed leaves on the forest floor are ideal for incubating their eggs. These "stump-tailed" and leaf chameleons are difficult to detect among the leaves, being camouflaged both by color and shape. At just 1.38 inches (3.5 cm) long the tiny *Brookesia peyrierasi* looks like a thin piece of wood when back and underside. The crest can be exaggerated and fanlike as in the sail-fin chameleon, *Chamaeleo montium* from West Africa. Others, such as *C. hoehnelii*, have a raised casque, giving it its common name of high-casqued chameleon. (It also has a distinctive upturned snout.)

Two rather strange species are *Chamaeleo xenorhinus* and *C. carpenteri* from Central Africa. The males have a large crest on top of the head and a huge rostral process. In Pfeffer's chameleon, *C. pfefferi* from Cameroon, both sexes have a gular (throat) crest made of elongated soft "spines." In Jackson's chameleon, *C. jacksonii* from Africa and Hawaii, the males use their horns in combat—they can be interlocked to twist a rival from its branch.

Prehensile Tails

Chameleons have prehensile tails (but in *Brookesia* and *Rhampholeon* the tail is only slightly prehensile). They are particularly useful for animals living in trees. They can be coiled around twigs to provide an anchor when extending the tongue or reaching out to grasp a branch. When covering any distance, chameleons can extend the tail for balance. In many species it is coiled up during rest or sleep. Falling chameleons have been seen to use the tail as a "brake" by grasping a branch with it. On each foot opposing groups of toes have become fused to produce feet that can grasp too, often with remarkable strength.

Chameleons spend much of their time motionless, their eyes constantly searching for prey or danger. Movement is usually slow and deliberate, but certain species can move surprisingly quickly when necessary. For example, when it feels threatened, *Furcifer lateralis* from Madagascar will climb rapidly and even leap from branch to branch to avoid being caught.

⊕ *Chameleons rely heavily on sight for feeding and during courtship. The flap-necked chameleon,* Chamaeleo dilepis, *shows the typically protruding eyes that can swivel independently, giving panoramic vision.*

Senses

A chameleon's eyes can move independently, giving all-round vision. The eyes protrude and, except for a relatively small area, are covered with skin. Small eyes probably help the chameleon remain concealed. When prey is spotted, accurate binocular vision enables it to judge the distance. The chameleon then shoots out its extensible tongue, and the prey "sticks" to it.

⊖ *The West African male sail-fin chameleons,* Chamaeleo montium, *have long rostral horns projecting straight forward along the lower snout. The females lack these horns and have only "horn buds."*

It appears that chameleons have little or no sense of smell. In other reptiles smell is detected by the Jacobson's organ in the roof of the mouth. In chameleons this organ is reduced and (as far as is known) is nonfunctional. Chameleons often press their tongue against branches (a technique referred to as "tongue testing"), but the reason for this is unclear. Some scientists think it may be a means of detecting the scent of other chameleons from fecal traces using a small organ with two "lobes" on the end of the tongue. When the tongue is extended to trap prey, the end is formed into a bulbous shape; but when lapping water, the tongue is flattened, and the "lobes" can be seen as small tendrils.

Chameleons have no voice as such. In confrontations a faint hiss may be heard, but it is probably an involuntary expulsion of air as the body is flattened. A similar hiss is sometimes heard when the tongue is retracted with prey attached. The veiled chameleon, *Chamaeleo calyptratus* from Yemen and Saudi Arabia, can produce a loud, hoarse hissing sound. Hearing is practically nonexistent in chameleons. Unlike most other lizards, they have no external ear opening. They can, however, detect airborne vibrations by means of a membrane on each side of the skull. This membrane is connected with the inner ear.

The Use of Color

Chameleons have special skin cells (chromatophores) that contain red and yellow pigments and that can shrink or expand. Together with a reflective layer and special cells containing a dark pigment (melanophores), they cause the skin to change color, sometimes extremely quickly.

Most chameleons are various shades of green and brown, which helps conceal them in trees. There is a mistaken belief that chameleons can change to any color to match their surroundings. But color is used mostly as a form of communication, and color changes are usually related to making the chameleon more visible in order to attract a mate, threaten a rival (or predator), and in the case of females, to warn off unwelcome suitors or intruding females. Males are highly territorial and will subject any intruder to aggressive displays combined with battle coloration. Gravid females (ones that are full of

Chameleon Myths

The Malagasy believe that the devil made chameleons from parts of other animals—the tail of a monkey, the skin of a crocodile, the tongue of a toad, and the horns of a rhinoceros.

During a period of prolonged drought in Central Africa a village chief sent a chameleon to the gods to ask for rain and save the people. But it moved so slowly that the message was only delivered after the people had died.

In Madagascar killing a chameleon is *fady* (taboo). They believe that if any injury is inflicted on *Brookesia* chameleons, the same will happen to the perpetrator. This has led the Malagasy to believe that chameleons have supernatural powers.

In Morocco dried chameleon is thought to act as a powerful medicine for humans, curing many illnesses.

eggs or young) exhibit spectacular color and pattern combinations. Female *Furcifer lateralis* display colors of white, red, yellow, light blue, black, and purple. No doubt they act as an effective warning to males, but they are no aid to concealment. In the lesser chameleon, *F. minor*, gravid females have particularly brilliant coloration (black with red, blue, and yellow scales). When compared with a male, they could easily be mistaken for a different species.

Color can be an indicator of health. A sick chameleon usually turns a sickly, yellowish shade. Color changes also relate to temperature. A cold chameleon is usually dark, often almost black. Specimens basking in the early morning sun can be dark on the exposed side (to absorb heat) with normal coloration on the other side. When it is very hot, chameleons often turn a lighter color before seeking shade among leaves. They probably gain more protection from their habit of resting motionless than from cryptic coloration. When they do move along a branch, it is usually with a jerky, swaying gait, possibly imitating the action of a leaf in the wind.

Feeding and Diet

While some chameleons eat vertebrates such as lizards, frogs, small mammals, and small birds, most enjoy a natural diet of live insects. When hungry, chameleons may stalk their prey. However, their usual method is to sit

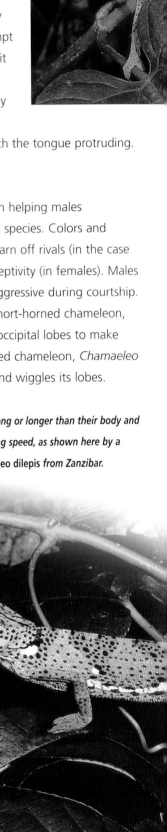

patiently and pick off any insects that come within reach of their long, extensible tongue. With this method the chameleon only has to move a minimal distance—a real advantage for a creature that lives among trees and bushes, and is unable to make a quick dash to seize prey.

The chameleon's tongue is a remarkable organ. Rather than being "sticky," it works more like a rubber sucker and needs to be moist in order to stick to the target. In some species the fully extended tongue can be almost twice the length of the body. Accelerator muscles in the tongue squeeze together to propel it from the mouth. The contractile muscles are elastic; after the tongue hits the insect, they contract to bring it back into the mouth. When not in use, the tongue is folded concertina-style in the mouth. Occasionally a chameleon might seize prey in its jaws if it appears too large to stick to the tongue or if the tongue has missed the insect once or twice and it is near enough to be grabbed.

Defense

Chameleons use various tactics when threatened. Many species have cryptic coloration, which makes hiding in trees and bushes effective. Stump-tailed chameleons combine this with "freezing" (remaining motionless until the danger has passed). Once spotted by a predator,

it is difficult for the chameleon to escape. However, by jumping from one branch to another or falling to the ground, some chameleons manage to elude their attacker. Occasionally a chameleon will hiss, inflate its gular pouch, and sway with its mouth open in an attempt to fool the enemy into thinking it is larger and fiercer than it is. Some chameleons feign death by lying sideways on a branch or hanging beneath the branch with the tongue protruding.

Reproduction

Vision and color are important in helping males distinguish females of their own species. Colors and patterns can be intensified to warn off rivals (in the case of males) or to signal sexual receptivity (in females). Males are territorial and can be very aggressive during courtship. To intimidate a rival male, the short-horned chameleon, *Calumma brevicornis,* raises its occipital lobes to make itself look bigger. The flap-necked chameleon, *Chamaeleo dilepis* from Africa, also raises and wiggles its lobes.

⊕ *Chameleons' tongues are often as long or longer than their body and can be shot out of the mouth at lightning speed, as shown here by a female flap-necked chameleon,* Chamaeleo dilepis *from Zanzibar.*

⊕ *In pursuit of a female a male flap-necked chameleon,* Chamaeleo dilepis, *picks its way along the branch of a tree on the island of Zanzibar. The species shows an obvious example of sexual dichromatism.*

Identifying the sex of many species of chameleons is relatively easy in mature specimens. As a general rule, it is the male that sports some kind of ornamentation such as horns, nasal appendages, casques, crests, or tarsal spurs. Occasionally a female may have some of these features, but they tend to be smaller than those of the male. Nasal appendages are usually a male feature, but in *Calumma nasuta* from Madagascar both sexes have one. However, the male's is wider and more rounded at the end.

A number of Madagascan chameleons exhibit sexual dichromatism (the males and females have different colors and patterns). *Furcifer labordi* males are green with white stripes on the flanks, while the females have red coloration on the throat, two small, red lateral markings on the neck, and a bluish color on the flanks.

Male chameleons initiate mating by rhythmic head movements and by intensifying their color. A receptive female stays quiet and does not change color. If she does not rebuff him, he mounts and aligns their cloacae, curling his tail under hers. Mating can take from a couple of minutes to almost an hour. After mating, females change color to show they are no longer "available."

As with all reptiles, chameleons can be divided into two reproductive groups—those that lay eggs and those whose eggs stay in the body until the young hatch (live-bearers). In the latter the young are fully formed and move off almost immediately. There is no dependence on the mother after birth. Gestation varies from four to seven months depending on species and temperatures. Gravid females often seek out warmer areas and spend more time basking. The young emerge still encased in a membrane (sac), or they may already have broken out from the membrane before emerging. The two-lined chameleon, *Chamaeleo bitaeniatus*, and *Bradypodion* females move along the branches depositing "complete" youngsters that cling to the branch. In *C. ellioti* the young are contained in a sac. Some fall onto branches, while others fall to the ground. Each sac contains an amount of fluid that gathers in the lower end and seems to act as a shock absorber. Within seconds of birth the youngsters pierce the membrane, emerge, and climb into the branches.

In egg-laying species the eggs develop in the female's oviduct. About six to eight weeks after mating, the female descends to the ground and digs a hole. After laying her eggs in the hole, she fills it in and tamps down the surface to obscure signs of nesting. This helps prevent predation by other animals. Eggs of some Madagascan species experience a diapause, a period during which development is suspended. It usually coincides with cooler temperatures and results in a longer incubation time. Eggs of Parson's chameleon, *Calumma parsonii*, can take up to 21 months to hatch. Depending on seasonal variations, they can have one or more diapauses.

Chameleon eggs have leathery shells that absorb moisture throughout the incubation period and increase in size. When they are ready to hatch, the youngsters make several slits at either end of the eggs, sufficient to allow the head to emerge. Full emergence does not take place until all the yolk has been absorbed, which may take as little as one hour or as much as two days. Hatching frequently takes place during a wet period, since the ground is softer, and it is easier for the youngsters to dig their way to the surface. Most chameleon babies are usually brown—this coloration gives them effective camouflage on branches and twigs.

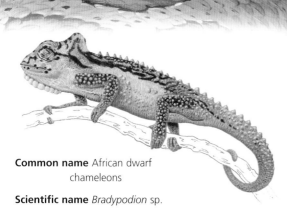

Common name African dwarf chameleons

Scientific name *Bradypodion* sp.

Family Chamaeleonidae

Suborder Sauria

Order Squamata

Number of species 21

Size From 4.5 in (11 cm) to 8 in (20 cm)

Key features Crests of small tubercles present along the back and throat; larger tubercles on body, legs, and tail; small to medium casque; faint dorsal and gular crests; females, juveniles, and males are usually mottled greens and browns in color outside the breeding season; displaying males can be spectacular; *Bradypodion* sp. differ from other chameleons in that they have single-lobed lungs

Habits Arboreal, climbing to the top of vegetation to bask; nights spent in denser vegetation for safety and warmth

Breeding Live-bearers; females produce 3 litters a year with about 12–15 babies in each litter; gestation lasts 3–5 months depending on species; species living at higher altitudes have the longer gestation period

Diet A wide variety of crawling and flying insects

Habitat From montane forest to coastal fynbos that offer grass, heathers, and low bushes; some species inhabit parks and gardens

Distribution South Africa

Status Setaro's dwarf chameleon, *Bradypodion setaroi*—Endangered (IUCN); Smith's dwarf chameleon, *B. taeniabronchum*—Critical (IUCN); others common locally

Similar species None

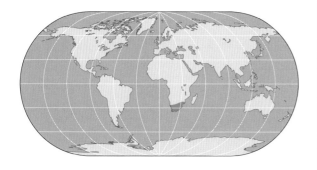

African Dwarf Chameleons

Bradypodion sp.

Bradypodion *species are unusual among chameleons in that they give birth to live young rather than lay eggs. Identification of species is difficult, but each is confined to and named after the specific locality in which it occurs.*

FOR SEVERAL YEARS there has been confusion over the exact number of species and subspecies within the genus *Bradypodion,* but it is now generally accepted that there are 21 species. They are sometimes divided roughly into two groups. First, there are the larger species, which are found predominantly in montane forests in Natal, Cape, and Transvaal. The second group, consisting of the smaller species, inhabits fynbos vegetation and coastal scrub areas. Old texts dealing with chameleons may use the name *Chamaeleo pumilus* to include all species or the name *Microsaura* when referring to the genus.

Temperature Control

Many regions inhabited by *Bradypodion* species experience relatively cold winters. During cold spells the chameleons bask on sunny days, but their activity levels fall. In evergreen areas they retreat into deep foliage, and in other areas they descend to the floor to find warmth and protection among leaf litter. All *Bradypodion* species flatten their bodies and turn dark to absorb heat. To avoid overheating, they retreat into shrubs and trees. They also adopt pale coloration to reflect heat and open their mouth to gape and lose heat. At night their heart slows down, and they turn a grayish color. This helps conserve heat during the colder nights.

Bradypodion damaranum, the Knysna dwarf chameleon, climbs high into the canopy to sleep in the center of ferns, its coiled tail resembling a newly emerging fern frond. Rain does not seem to affect this small chameleon. It takes advantage of it by lapping water from

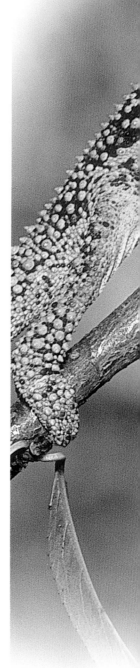

↑ *The Natal midlands dwarf chameleon,* **Bradypodion thamnobates,** *comes from the South African province of Kwazulu-Natal. Its preferred habitat is in bushes and scrubs along roads, fences, and gardens.*

leaves. Like most chameleons, *Bradypodion* prefer to drink in the morning, since a moist tongue works better for catching prey.

Bradypodion means "slow foot," a good description, since all species in the genus have a hesitant stop-go gait that is particularly effective when stalking insects. Their jerky walk matches the movement of the foliage. Their diet changes according to season. For example, Smith's dwarf chameleon, *B. taeniabronchum,* moves into protea bushes when they begin to flower and feeds on flying insects attracted by the pollen. When the flowering season is over, it seeks another type of plant.

Breeding

Bradypodion breed for eight to nine months of the year. When defending territory or courting a female, the male's color intensifies, and he nods his head up and down several times in quick succession. A receptive female often allows a male to mate several times a day for a few days. This ensures that more live young and

Keeping a Low Profile

Predators of *Bradypodion* chameleons include the boomslang, *Dispholidus typus,* the spotted bush snake, *Philothamnus semivariegatus,* larger lizards, and the long-tailed shrike, *Corvinella melanoleuca,* which impales the chameleons on a spike or large thorn before eating them. Since some species in the genus have adapted to urban parks and gardens, dogs and cats are also potential hazards. Some spiders prey on baby chameleons. The chameleons respond to threats by retreating slowly into foliage or "squirreling"—by swiveling around, they put the branch between themselves and the danger. If little foliage cover is available, they drop into the leaf litter. Occasionally a specimen will make an aggressive show by expanding its gular pouch and bobbing its head, which is not very effective against its enemies.

fewer unfertilized ova are produced. Gravid females are intolerant of other chameleons, including members of their own sex.

Bradypodion bear live young. The eggs continue developing in the female's body, which is important for creatures living in areas with temperatures that fluctuate. Low temperatures at night would kill off eggs incubating in soil; but inside the female they stay warm, and development is not slowed down. Females give birth 90 to 150 days after mating. As they are born, the babies break out of the membrane and are deposited on a branch.

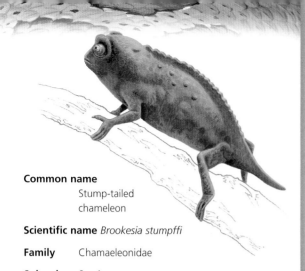

Common name
Stump-tailed chameleon

Scientific name *Brookesia stumpffi*

Family Chamaeleonidae

Suborder Sauria

Order Squamata

Size 3.5 in (9 cm) long

Key features Skull triangular shaped; tail relatively short compared with other genera and only faintly prehensile; curved crest over eye; body elongated; dorsal crest made up of paired spiny scales; legs and casque have pointed sharp scales; there is a plate over the base of the tail that extends onto each side; color brownish gray or green

Habits Diurnal, spending most of the time hunting insects in leaf litter; becomes more active during the rainy season

Breeding Females lay up to 2 clutches a year, usually in January or February; each clutch contains 2 or sometimes 4 eggs; eggs hatch after 6–8 weeks

Diet Insects such as small flies, termites, small beetles, and young mantids

Habitat Leaf litter and vegetation up to 39 in (100 cm) from the ground

Distribution North and northwestern Madagascar, including the island of Nosy Bé

Status Common

Similar species *Brookesia ebenaui* and *B. superciliaris*

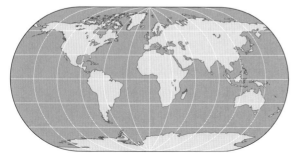

Stump-Tailed Chameleon

Brookesia stumpffi

Despite (or perhaps because of) its tiny size, Brookesia stumpffi *has mastered the art of defense. It uses a range of techniques to protect itself from predators in its forest habitat.*

BROOKESIA STUMPFFI IS ONE of 23 species of stump-tailed chameleons that are endemic to Madagascar. All the species are small—from 1.38 to 4.25 inches (3.5–11 cm). They are terrestrial and have cryptic, usually brownish coloration. Their tails are relatively short, and on land they are used as a support rather than a gripping aid as in other chameleons.

Brookesia stumpffi is the commonest of all these small chameleons. It inhabits both primary and secondary forests, and has also colonized abandoned coffee plantations. Within its area temperatures are usually warm, ranging from 73 to 82°F (23–28°C), although the forest floor is a little cooler. During the rainy seasons (October to November and March to April) humidity reaches 85 percent. If the temperature drops too low, the chameleons hibernate; if it rises too high, they estivate.

The ability to tolerate a wide range of conditions has enabled *B. stumpffi* to inhabit both wet and dry deciduous forests, where leaf litter is always present. Because they live in leaf litter, *Brookesia* chameleons do not experience a wide daily variation in temperature (unlike many other species of chameleon) and do not need to bask in the mornings to become functional.

Camouflage

In common with other members of the genus, *B. stumpffi* has only a limited ability to change color from pale to dark brown. Body coloration in these chameleons is used mainly for defense and camouflage rather than for display. If disturbed, they darken rapidly and can produce blotched brown markings on their sides that help disrupt their body shape against dead leaves. Interestingly, unlike other chameleons, *Brookesia* chameleons do not turn white just before shedding their skin. Nor do they become pale at night (unlike the western pygmy chameleons, *Rhampholeon* species).

Brookesia stumpffi uses the last bit of daylight to climb into vegetation and spends the night clinging to a twig or leaf with its head pointing down. Roosting in this way prevents predation by hedgehoglike tenrecs, which are nocturnal foragers, since the thin stems will not bear the weight of a tenrec.

Defensive Postures

Of all the stump-tailed chameleons, *B. stumpffi* shows the widest range of defensive postures. Most *Brookesia* species freeze

⊕ *Like all stump-tailed chameleons,* **Brookesia superciliaris** *from Madagascar has warm, earthy coloration and an unusual body shape that provide the perfect camouflage for the forest undergrowth.*

when disturbed, but *B. stumpffi* walks fast when it senses danger. Its second line of defense is to become immobile and flatten its back, so that when viewed from above, it resembles a leaf—a useful technique if the predator is a bird. If that fails and the chameleon is grabbed, its body vibrates, surprising the predator and causing it to release the chameleon. (A similar defense mechanism is used by *Rhampholeon* species.) *Brookesia stumpffi* has a fourth defensive tactic known as spine thrusting. When it twists its body, the line of spines running along the dorsal crest is thrust outward. This causes discomfort or even pain to the predator's mouth, and it releases the chameleon.

Courtship Displays

Brookesia stumpffi is a solitary creature. If it sees another member of its own species, it adopts a gaping mouth and a swaying movement. Males fight and try to push each other over.

When a male detects a female, he does not display threat behavior. Instead, he adopts a mottled coloration resembling lichen and bobs his head up and down. Unreceptive females shake their heads. Mating pairs roost together until all mating activity, which usually takes place in the evening, has ceased. As with western pygmy chameleons, *Rhampholeon* species, stump-tails lay their eggs in leaf litter. The eggs of *B. stumpffi* seem quite large for such a small species, measuring 0.6 x 0.4 inches (14 x 10 mm). With the constant temperature and humidity of the forest floor the eggs hatch about six to eight weeks later. The young measure 1.3 inches (3.3 cm) and reach sexual maturity at five months.

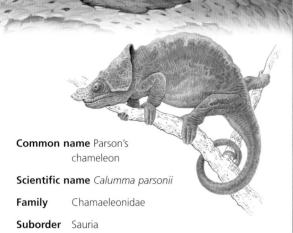

Common name Parson's chameleon

Scientific name *Calumma parsonii*

Family Chamaeleonidae

Suborder Sauria

Order Squamata

Size Usually up to 24 in (60 cm) long

Key features Males have paired, warty rostral processes; both sexes have occipital lobes (flaps) at the back of the head; no dorsal or ventral crest; male coloration is turquoise-blue with yellow or orange eyes; females are a uniform green; the casque and forehead are brown; 4 or 5 darker diagonal lines break up the coloration on the flanks; both sexes have a pale yellow or white spot in the center of the flanks

Habits Slow moving, inactive for most of the day; remains in one place if temperatures are within its requirements, and water and food are available; does not like to bask for extended periods; prefers filtered sunlight

Breeding Females lay 1 clutch of 40–60 eggs per year; eggs take about 21–23 months to hatch

Diet Large insects such as grasshoppers, butterflies, moths, stick and leaf insects, cockroaches; also small mammals and birds

Habitat Rain forests; prefers primary (untouched) forest with cool, humid conditions; it rarely adapts to secondary forest

Distribution There are isolated populations on the eastern coast of Madagascar; also northern Madagascar and the islands of Nosy Boraha and Nosy Bé (yellow-lipped form)

Status Common locally

Similar species *Calumma globifer* and *C. oshaughnessyi*

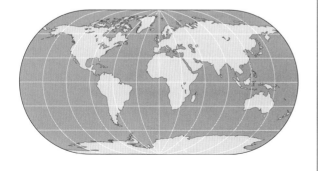

Parson's Chameleon

Calumma parsonii

Parson's chameleons are shy and have a laid-back approach to life. Their low metabolism combined with periods of inactivity enable them to cope with the low temperatures they sometimes encounter.

ITS SIZE AND COLORATION make Parson's chameleon an impressive creature. As a result of taxonomic changes, two subspecies of the chameleon are recognized from the eastern rain forest of Madagascar. *Calumma parsonii parsonii* is the more well-known turquoise-blue form; *C. p. cristifer*, which is less well known, is about 6 inches (15 cm) smaller. It has green coloration and a dorsal crest of small, regular tubercles. In both subspecies the scales are homogeneous (all the same size) and smooth.

Parson's chameleons are found at altitudes of 1,300 to 4,000 feet (400–1,200 m). On Madagascar the highest rainfall occurs on the eastern coast, and it decreases the farther west one goes. Similarly, the northern part of the island is wetter than the south.

They inhabit lowland evergreen and montane forest where temperatures are relatively cool, that is, below 82°F (28°C). The cool temperatures combined with high humidity produce cloud forests. Parson's chameleons prefer primary forest, but only a small percentage of dense original forest still remains untouched on Madagascar. The scarcity of suitable habitat and the fact that each male has a territory approaching 1 acre (0.4 ha) pose a threat to the continued existence of the species.

These chameleons have been called the sloths of the chameleon world. Their approach to feeding is to adopt a sit-and-wait technique. They are slow drinkers, often lapping leaves for 30 minutes or more. It is sometimes simply the need to defecate that makes them move, only to return to the same spot later.

Hibernation

The habitat of Parson's chameleons exhibits a wide range of temperatures. Due to altitudinal and seasonal variations temperatures can fall as low as 45°F (7°C) and rise to 82°F (28°C). The eastern coast experiences winters with a significant drop in temperature. Parson's chameleons respond to this by entering a dormant, or hibernation, period. They have a lower metabolism than many chameleon species, which enables them to cope with low temperatures. They slow down the pace of life so that they undertake little activity for several weeks. Their intake of food and water also decreases accordingly.

⊙ *Among the largest of Madagascan chameleons, C. parsonii parsonii adult males have been known to reach nearly 30 inches (76 cm) long, including their tail.*

Parson's chameleons are shy creatures and are easily stressed by the presence of another chameleon or a predator. When stressed, the male's coloration lightens so that the darker stripes on its sides stand out. In addition, dark spots appear over all its body. Females intensify the yellow coloration to such an extent that they look like yellow chameleons with small green blotches. Stress coloration is not the only indicator of male-to-male aggression. Males also stand on straight legs and bring their tail over their back. They may also indulge in head butting until one or the other retreats.

Not only do males and females have different coloration (sexual dichromatism), they also have different features (dimorphism). The male has a longer tail with a thickened tail base and larger rostral processes than the female.

Breeding Activity

The trigger for breeding is the end of the hibernation, or dormant, period when temperatures begin to rise, and the chameleons return to normal levels of activity. The rise in temperature stimulates the chameleons into mating. With intense coloration and much head bobbing the male approaches the female; if she is receptive, mating can last for up to an hour. An unreceptive female flattens her body, displays yellow mottling, and rocks from side to side on the branch. She may even crash through the foliage onto a lower branch to escape from the male.

Temperatures are still low when she lays her eggs, so minimal development takes place at first. Several months at higher temperatures follow before the seasons change. Then the eggs undergo a second dormant, very cool period. In total, the eggs take 21–23 months to hatch. The newly emerged young measure 3 inches (8 cm) long. Unlike other chameleon species whose young are green or brown, which provides excellent camouflage, those of Parson's chameleons are yellowish orange. It is not known why they should be this color, since it cannot help with concealment.

Common name Namaqua chameleon

Scientific name *Chamaeleo namaquensis*

Family   Chamaeleonidae

Suborder   Sauria

Order   Squamata

Size   10 in (25 cm) long

Key features Head and mouth large; dorsal crest consisting of 14 knoblike tubercles that grow smaller toward the tail; tail not fully prehensile; gular crest lacking; color varies from dull yellowish gray to pinkish brown with scattered darker spots on the body; 5 large, pale spots form a lateral line along the sides of the body; background color varies depending on location—those from inland areas are pinkish brown to blend in with the color of the sand

Habits   Diurnal; terrestrial; spends the nights in burrows

Breeding   Female lays 2–3 clutches per year; clutch size varies from 6–22 eggs depending on the season; eggs hatch after 3–4 months

Diet   Beetles, insects (especially locusts), small snakes, lizards, and geckos

Habitat   Semiarid and desert areas, particularly sandy regions, coastal dunes, and scrub vegetation

Distribution Parts of South Africa, including western Cape Province, Namaqualand, the Namib Desert, and southern Angola

Status   Common

Similar species Common chameleon, *Chamaeleo chameleon*

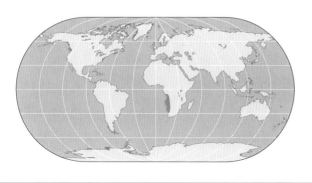

Namaqua Chameleon

Chamaeleo namaquensis

Living as it does in one of the world's most inhospitable regions, the Namaqua chameleon needs to be resilient. It is a fierce creature that can tackle even venomous snakes in its quest for survival.

THE NAMAQUA CHAMELEON is a terrestrial lizard that lives in some of the hottest and most desolate areas of South Africa. Part of its habitat includes the Namib Desert, a narrow coastal strip of shifting sand dunes where plant cover is sparse. Rainfall can be as low as 0.5 inches (10 mm) a year, and some years there is no rain. However, a cold offshore current causes moisture-laden fogs to drift across the dunes most mornings, depositing much-needed moisture on rocks, vegetation, and even the chameleon's body. The moisture is lapped up by the chameleons.

Namaqua chameleons use several tactics to capture food, including stealth and a sit-and-wait approach. They use their extensible tongue to reach out and capture prey. However, they will chase beetles and small lizards, and grab them in their jaws. They have also been seen flushing prey out of bushes and from under stones. They have a voracious appetite and will eat anything small enough to swallow. Foraging for small items at the seaside can result in too much salt building up in the chameleon's body, but a nasal salt gland excretes the excess.

Facing up to Predators

Monitor lizards, vipers, and birds of prey are the Namaqua chameleon's main enemies. Unlike arboreal chameleons, this species can run away relatively quickly from danger—traveling at up to 3 miles per hour (5 km/h). It has a fierce disposition and will face up to predators. It uses various means to deter potential enemies, including standing with legs fully extended, adopting black coloration, expanding its gular

→ *The Namaqua chameleon has the ability to change color in response to variations in light or temperature. Its body darkens to absorb more heat from the sun and lightens to cool off.*

pouch, hissing, and throwing open its mouth to reveal the yellow-orange lining. These warnings are often followed up with a forward thrust and a bite from its strong jaws.

Breeding

Males initiate courtship by approaching a female and using side-to-side head-bobbing movements. However, being larger than males, unreceptive females can inflict considerable damage on a potential mate. About six weeks after mating, the female prepares the nest site. It is often a deeper extension to her nighttime burrow, allowing her to guard the eggs from predators. Incubation takes between three and four months depending on temperature. The youngsters hatch during the cooler night and avoid the searing heat of the day that could dehydrate them. Even as hatchlings, the females are larger than the males.

The babies move off in search of small bushes. For the first few weeks they use the bush for shelter and as a feeding station; but as they grow, they adopt the more terrestrial lifestyle of the adults.

Venomous Prey

The small venomous Peringuey's adder, *Bitis peringueyi*, features on the Namaqua chameleon's menu. The chameleon uses its tongue to strike the snake on the head. It then crushes it in its jaws before the adder can deliver a lethal bite.

Heating and Cooling

Morning temperatures in the Namib can be close to freezing. The chameleons emerge from their burrows and angle their bodies to catch the sun's rays. They even inflate their gular pouch to absorb as much heat as quickly as possible. After a period they turn around to warm the other side of their body. An increase in body temperature is accompanied by color change from almost black to either yellowish gray or pinkish brown with darker spots. When it is cold and in its dark form, the Namaqua chameleon is vulnerable to predators.

Daytime temperatures can soar to 150°F (65°C). Once the temperature exceeds 105°F (40°C), the chameleons need to take action to avoid overheating. As well as looking for shade under bushes, they gape their mouth to allow heat to dissipate. To reduce the cooling effects of winds, they shelter in grooves in the dunes and catch the last rays of the sun. They spend the night in a burrow, often a rodent hole, since some warmth is retained there.

Common name Veiled chameleon
(Yemen chameleon)

Scientific name *Chamaeleo calyptratus*

Family   Chamaeleonidae

Suborder   Sauria

Order   Squamata

Size   From 16 in (41 cm) to 20 in (50 cm) long

Key features High, laterally compressed casque; scales of
different sizes; coloration of males consists of
light yellow bands alternating with bluish-
green bands; gular area and underside paler
bluish green; females light green; both sexes
have a row of white patches on both sides

Habits   Sun loving and more heat tolerant than most
other species of chameleons

Breeding   Female lays up to 3 clutches a year, each
containing 12–20 eggs; eggs hatch after 6–8
months

Diet   Large insects (grasshoppers, locusts, spiders),
small lizards and geckos, small mammals, and
plant matter

Habitat   Mountainous regions, dry forested areas in
valleys, and riverbeds with oases; areas range
from lush, semitropical vegetation to arid
deserts

Distribution San'a and Dhamer in western Yemen; the
subspecies *Chamaeleo calyptratus calcarifer*
occurs along the southwestern coast of Saudi
Arabia

Status   Common

Similar species None

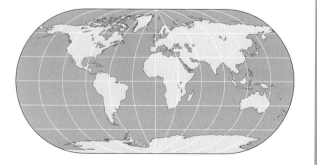

LIZARDS

Veiled Chameleon

Chamaeleo calyptratus

*The combination of bluish-green and yellow bands
and an unusually high casque combine to make the
veiled chameleon a most impressive creature.*

THE HABITAT OF THE VEILED CHAMELEON ranges from
humid low coastal plains to mountain slopes
that receive rain six months of the year to
plateaus 12,000 feet (3,660 m) high with hardly
any rainfall. The virtually treeless high plateaus
also experience severe night frosts; in order to
avoid them, the chameleons crawl into rocky
crevices. The mountain slopes are cultivated and
attract a wide variety of insects. Temperatures
there rarely exceed 86°F (30°C). Such ideal
conditions have led to larger numbers of veiled
chameleons in these areas. Where land has
been irrigated for agriculture or to provide
gardens in towns, veiled chameleons have taken
advantage of the additional habitats.

On the high plateaus winters are dry and
cold. The veiled chameleons living there spend
the early morning warming up until their body
temperature is high enough to begin feeding
activities. When the temperature reaches 114°F
(45.5°C), the chameleons show thermal
stress—they gape their mouth and seek shade
where possible. In order to conserve moisture in
such an arid environment, they do not excrete
urine as a liquid. Intead, they have nasal salt
glands that allow them to excrete sodium and
potassium as a concentrated white powder
without losing moisture. This can be seen as
white deposits around their nostrils.

Omnivorous Animals

They are unusual among chameleons in that
they consume some plant matter to supplement
their diet of insects, lizards, and geckos,
especially in the dry season. By chewing the
leaves, they can extract valuable moisture.

The veiled chameleon is one of the
most aggressive chameleon species. When

Unusual Casque

The casque of the veiled chameleon is 3.5 to 4 inches (8–10 cm) high. It is used to collect moisture droplets from the morning dew, which then run down into the animal's mouth—a useful trick in arid areas. It is also thought to be a fat supply for times when food is scarce.

The casque contains a large number of blood vessels that cool the chameleon's blood, thereby enabling it to reduce its temperature during the hotter months of the year. The flaps on either side of the casque can be pulled forward, making the head look larger and the chameleon appear more intimidating.

threatened, it responds by intensifying its colors. It also expands its gular pouch and stands sideways to look larger, while curling and uncurling the tail and hissing.

Normally veiled chameleons are intolerant of others nearby. However, in areas where trees are scarce, they have developed an unusual pyramid type of housing. A mature male lays claim to the top of the tree, lower down are females, and on the lowest branches are young males. Hatchlings tend to perch in tall grass.

Breeding

Veiled chameleons are sexually dimorphic in several ways: Males have a larger casque, females are smaller, and the two sexes show different color patterns. The males, even as hatchlings, have a tarsal spur on the heel of their hind feet.

In the wild clutch sizes vary between 12 and 20 eggs. However, under optimum conditions in captivity clutch sizes can reach up to 80. Female veiled chameleons also have the ability to store sperm, so two consecutive clutches can be produced from a single mating.

The egg-laying site consists of a tunnel dug at an angle of 45 degrees to the ground, often under the roots of bushes or trees where the earth is soft and easy to dig. After six to eight months the eggs hatch simultaneously rather than being staggered over a period of several days. This strategy probably increases the survival rate of hatchlings, but it also enables the young to help each other dig their way to the surface.

↩ *Veiled chameleons are distinctive-looking animals with a proportionately high, narrow casque that is used for collecting precious moisture.*

71

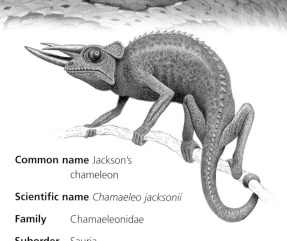

Common name Jackson's chameleon

Scientific name *Chamaeleo jacksonii*

Family Chamaeleonidae

Suborder Sauria

Order Squamata

Size 12 in (30 cm) long

Key features 3 horns present on the head—2 at eye level (orbital), the 3rd located on the tip of the snout (rostral) and curving upward; dorsal crest of prominent tubercles gives the impression of a saw blade; female's horns much reduced or absent; basic coloration green; small crest to the rear of the head is outlined by conical scales

Habits Solitary, each with its own territory; individuals from middle elevations hold their body perpendicular to sun's rays to warm up in the morning; color changes to yellow when it becomes too warm; moves into deep foliage for shade and to begin feeding

Breeding Live-bearer; female produces 1 or 2 clutches each year; each clutch contains up to 35 young; gestation period about 6–9 months

Diet Insects, particularly grasshoppers, butterflies, katydids, spiders, and flies

Habitat High altitudes; found at elevations of 8,000 ft (2,440 m) that have high rainfall and distinct wet and dry seasons leading to fluctuations in temperature and humidity; common in primary and secondary forest

Distribution Mountains of Kenya and Tanzania (East Africa); introduced to Hawaii

Status Common

Similar species *Chamaeleo johnstonii* (although this species is an egg layer)

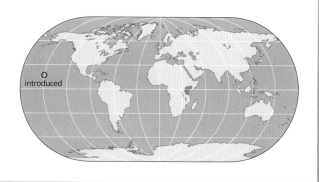

introduced

Jackson's Chameleon

Chamaeleo jacksonii

Jackson's chameleons are found on the African continent, predominantly on the highlands of Kenya and Tanzania. The three-horned males look like miniature Triceratops.

OF ALL THE THREE-HORNED CHAMELEONS, Jackson's is the best known. There are three subspecies— *C. j. jacksonii*, *C. j. merumantana*, and *C. j. xantholophus*. The main differences between the subspecies relate to size, with *C. j. xantholophus* being the largest and *C. j. merumantana* the smallest. There is also variation in the females' horns (or lack of them) depending on subspecies. *Chamaeleo j. xantholophus* is often described as the most attractive of the three forms. It has a yellow crest and yellow on the ridge at the back of its head. In the past Jackson's chameleon has been confused with Johnston's chameleon, *Chamaeleo johnstonii*, an egg layer from the mountains of Burundi, Rwanda, and Zaire.

Jackson's chameleon's habitat in the mountains of East Africa is moderately cool with high humidity. Although rainfall exceeds 50 inches (127 cm) per year, there are distinct wet and dry seasons. Daytime temperatures reach 80°F (27°C), and an average nighttime temperature is 59°F (15°C), although it can drop to as low as 42°F (5°C). Human population explosion in Kenya and Tanzania has led to the felling of considerable tracts of primary forest; as a result, Jackson's chameleon has adapted to living in secondary forest and plantations, the latter being particularly rich in insect life. In fact, plantations have the highest population density of Jackson's chameleons.

Color and Defense

The basic coloration of Jackson's chameleon is a uniform green to yellow-brown with pale blotches forming a faint lateral line. This lichenlike coloring provides excellent

⊕ The horns on male Jackson's chameleons are not just ornamental. These two males have locked horns in a ritualized shoving contest over a mating territory.

camouflage among foliage. Juveniles are dark green, almost black, with white triangular markings on either side of the dorsal crest that serve to break up their outline.

When a threat from a bird is perceived, the chameleon moves deeper into the foliage where the bird cannot follow. An alternative defense strategy is to relax its grip on the branch, fall to the ground, and move to the base of a shrub. If it detects a threat from other predators, such as venomous and nonvenomous tree snakes, it responds by flattening the sides of its body and darkening its color. The mouth gapes, and the chameleon swings its head around in an attempt to bite.

Breeding

While breeding males intensify their colors, those of receptive females become lighter. Following a successful mating, the female gains weight. She tends to stop feeding for several weeks prior to giving birth as the developing young take up more room. The gestation period varies depending on temperature. Gravid females spend more time basking, angling their body so that the underneath of the body gets the sun's rays. They give birth to live young, usually in the morning. The young emerge from the female's cloaca, each encased in a membrane that is deposited on a branch and from which the baby breaks free. They disperse among the foliage and catch their own food within hours.

Horns

The horns of Jackson's chameleons are not collected for use in traditional medicine, but many East Africans regard cutting off a chameleon's horn as an act of great courage.

Male Jackson's chameleons engage in combat, locking horns and using them to try to force their opponent off the branch. Larger horns are obviously an advantage, since an individual can inflict damage on its opponent without receiving any.

Hawaiian Habitat

In 1981 the Kenyan government halted the previous widescale export of Jackson's chameleons, but the owner of a pet store on the Hawaiian island of Oahu obtained a permit to import a few specimens. Because they arrived in poor condition, they were released into a garden to try to improve them. They found the climate similar to that of their native habitat in East Africa, and from this initial group scattered populations of Jackson's chameleon have become established on the islands of Oahu and Maui.

Common name Panther chameleon

Scientific name *Furcifer pardalis*

Family Chamaeleonidae

Suborder Sauria

Order Squamata

Size From 15 in (38 cm) to 22 in (56 cm) long depending on locality; female a little smaller

Key features Males and females differ in color, shape, and size; male has a prominent rostral ridge (less prominent in female); snout bears enlarged scales; males vary from blue to green to pink depending on location; females grayish fawn or light pinkish brown; both sexes have a lateral line of whitish or bluish oval blotches

Habits Lives on small shrubs or even weeds in deforested areas; on cool days it basks, on warm days it sits in partial shade

Breeding Female lays 2–4 clutches a year; clutch size 12–45 eggs; eggs hatch after 6–13 months

Diet Large insects, small mammals, small lizards and geckos; in some localities small frogs are eaten

Habitat Forest edge; agricultural and suburban areas

Distribution Eastern coast and coastal islands of northern and eastern Madagascar; small populations on Reunion Island and Mauritius

Status Common

Similar species None

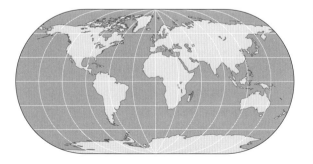

Panther Chameleon *Furcifer pardalis*

Numerous local myths surround the panther chameleon, probably due to the fact that it is not only common and conspicuous but also very colorful.

THE NATURAL RANGE OF PANTHER CHAMELEONS is the northern half of Madagascar. They occur from sea level to 3,900 feet (1,200 m), and the areas they inhabit are wet for eight months of the year. The northeastern part of their range receives 140 inches (355 cm) of rain a year, although there is progressively less rainfall the farther west and south one goes. Temperatures range from a daytime high of 96°F (35°C) to 50°F (10°C) at night during winter months, but frosts are restricted to the highest mountain peaks. Generally speaking, the climate is warm and humid with some seasonal fluctuations.

Panther chameleons dislike areas of deep shade. They prefer forest edge, agricultural fields, and suburban gardens. They are frequently seen in towns, crossing roads and moving from one garden to another. When using trees, they perch in the crown, but bushes up to 10 feet (3 m) high are their favorite perching places. Unlike many other species of chameleon, panther chameleons actually benefit from human disturbance: When an area of forest is cleared revealing shrubby undergrowth, they move in. They bask in the early morning sunlight to raise their body temperature; once they reach the optimum temperature, they move to perches in filtered sunlight.

Color Variants

More than any other species, male panther chameleons demonstrate geographical variation in color. Males from the island of Nosy Bé are light emerald-green or blue-green with yellow lips or uniformly turquoise-blue (sometimes referred to as the blue phase). Those from

 SEE ALSO Chameleons 44:56

Panther Chameleon Myths

everal myths surround the panther chameleon. For example, the Malagasy believe that killing one, even accidentally, will bring bad luck to the person responsible. So strong is the belief that it is possible to see drivers swerve dangerously to avoid panther chameleons that are crossing the road.

Touching or eating a panther chameleon is forbidden, especially for women—it is thought that their babies will be born dead. This is possibly linked to the first myth, but the vivid coloration of the panther chameleons leads the Malagasy to believe they are poisonous.

Because they see these chameleons falling out of bushes or trees at certain times of the year, the Malagasy people believe that the panther chameleons are committing suicide. However, this phenomenon usually coincides with the dry season when food becomes scarce. The panthers are therefore forced into closer contact with each other, and in order to avoid fights, some fall either to the ground or onto lower branches.

Maroansetra and Tamatave regions are green with a light blue to gray dorsal crest and are capable of changing to a bright orange-red in a few seconds.

There are two color forms from Ambanja. Some males have a dark green body with vertical red bands. The other color form from the area is a blue panther, a stunning creature with a turquoise-blue body, head, and legs and with dark blue vertical bands. In contrast, its eye turrets are orange.

In the Diego Suarez region males are green with blue bands; when stressed, their body color changes from green to yellow, and the vertical bands turn red. Recently a pink form has been found at Ankaramy. Normal coloration of the Ankaramy form is grayish pink with pale turquoise vertical bands, legs, and head. The lateral line is yellow. When this creature becomes stressed, the background color turns pink, and the vertical bands, legs, and head become almost purple.

Geographical color variations among young female panthers have not been studied to the

⊖ *No chameleon shows more geographical color variation than the panther chameleons. Note the opposed toes in this male, a useful aid for gripping.*

same extent as in the males, but their colors are more subtle, varying from fawn to grayish fawn and light pinkish brown.

Social Displays

Panther chameleons are probably the most common and conspicuous chameleons in Madagascar. They are also among the most territorial. During male-to-male exchanges males undergo rapid color change, and their bodies are compressed from side to side. As a result, the ventral surface and gular pouch are extended. They curl their tail, and their eye turrets change color. One male moves slowly toward its rival; if it does not retreat, a bout of head pushing begins. Their strong jaws can tear flesh and break bones. If a panther is seriously injured, death is inevitable.

In male-to-female exchanges the males color up in the same way as when fighting a rival, but the color change is accompanied by vertical head bobbing. When nongravid females encounter each other, there is no change from their normal subdued coloration. Gravid (egg-bearing) females, however, are intolerant of all males and females, and they turn dark brown

⊕ ⊖ Color differences in panther chameleons reflect not only local variations but also the animal's response to danger or courtship advances. Above left: a blue-phase male from Nosy Bé. Above right: Young female showing coloration prior to becoming sexually active. Right: The face and legs of stressed males often turn red.

with contrasting salmon-pink blotches on the lateral line. They extend their gular pouch, which shows bright red markings.

Breeding

The length of the breeding season varies from place to place. For example, in Nosy Bé females produce four clutches a year, but in Ambanja and Diego Suarez they only produce two. The reason is that the seasons become more pronounced the farther south one travels within the range of the panther chameleon. In Nosy Bé there is little temperature fluctuation, and humidity is relatively high for most of the year.

Males can be a little too zealous when approaching a female for mating. Unreceptive females often resort to biting to subdue an overamorous male. Female panthers become receptive as soon as they reach maturity, which can be as early as four months old. (During the breeding season they become receptive again about two to three weeks after laying a clutch.) The female indicates that she is receptive by turning a uniform pale salmon color. Females are receptive for four to five days. Gravid females usually choose to lay their eggs in the root system of shrubs and trees, since the ground there is less compact. The roots attract moisture, so the eggs will not dehydrate.

Incubation Times

Panther chameleons, as well as other species from Madagascar, lay eggs that are at a very early stage of development. In some parts of their range the eggs are laid just before a cooler, drier period—the winter. Development is suspended for one to three months (depending on the region), and the eggs undergo what is known as a diapause. When normal temperatures resume, development continues. This increases the overall incubation period to between 11 and 13 months. However, in areas with minimal seasonal temperature fluctuations the eggs do not undergo a diapause; instead, they hatch after six to eight months. The length of the diapause varies from region to region. The hatchlings seem quite tiny for such a large species, measuring just 1.5 inches (3.8 cm) long.

Common name Western pygmy chameleon
(leaf chameleon, African pygmy chameleon)

Scientific name *Rhampholeon spectrum*

Family   Chamaeleonidae

Suborder   Sauria

Order   Squamata

Size   3 in (8 cm) long

Key features Small rostral appendage (often mistaken for
a horn); slightly raised casque to rear of head;
dorsal crest made up of regular-shaped
tubercles; tail relatively short and only faintly
prehensile; lateral ridge along sides of body;
tiny spines on underside of feet; body color
brown with 2 diagonal black stripes

Habits   Spends most of the day on forest floor in leaf
litter, foraging for insects; at night perches on
branches 3 ft (91 cm) above the floor

Breeding   Female lays up to 4 clutches of 2–4 eggs per
year; eggs hatch after 6–8 weeks

Diet   Spiders, crickets, small cockroaches, termites

Habitat   Evergreen and semievergreen rain forest near
sea level and montane cloud forest up to
6,250 ft (1,900 m)

Distribution West Africa (Congo, Gabon, Equatorial
Guinea, and Cameroon)

Status   Common

Similar species *Rhampholeon affinis* and *R. boulengeri*

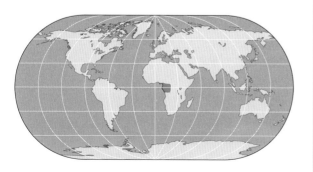

Western Pygmy Chameleon

Rhampholeon spectrum

*It is easy to overlook the little western pygmy
chameleon. With its dull brown colors it blends in well
against the background foliage and could be mistaken
for a dead leaf.*

THE WESTERN PYGMY chameleon is sometimes
referred to as the leaf chameleon. The scientific
name *Rhampholeon* means "crawling lion" and
refers to the fact that all species in the genus
have bicuspid claws on each toe (meaning that
each claw is crescent shaped and has two
points). The claws are used for gripping.

    Rhampholeon spectrum is quite unusual in
that its habitat encompasses a broad range of
altitudes from close to sea level up to about
6,250 feet (1,900 m). This means that the
western pygmy chameleon shares its habitat
with many lowland and montane species of
Chamaeleo. However, because the western
pygmy chameleon is primarily terrestrial and the
Chamaeleo species are arboreal, there is no
competition for food or territory.

Threatened Habitat?

The western pygmy chameleon prefers primary
forest with a considerable canopy and ground
cover with moist leaf litter. Where areas of
forest have been felled, it is less common, and it
is totally absent from farmland. Deforestation
for timber and agriculture is creating pockets of
habitat; since the western pygmy chameleon
seems to avoid severely degraded areas with
changes in forest-floor vegetation, it could
become locally threatened.

    These chameleons display cryptic (disguise)
coloration. They are usually brown with
between one and three diagonal black stripes
on the body. Occasionally specimens are found
in which the basic coloration varies from a dark
greenish brown to reddish brown. The ability to
change color is significantly less than in other

species of chameleons, but most specimens sport brighter colors at night. When stressed, females may intensify the red color, and males become pinkish white with diagonal black lines. Some specimens also allow moss to grow on their skin so they resemble a partly decaying leaf. Their color and pattern, together with a leaf-shaped body and slow, barely perceptible movements, provide excellent camouflage.

When males embark on territorial disputes with other males, they compress their bodies to about 0.25 inches (6 mm), and their color becomes paler. They sway from side to side, and they vibrate with the stress. The confrontation ends when one male backs down or is bitten. Nocturnal foraging snakes are their main enemy; in order to avoid such predators at night, they use dead or living shrub stems or even narrow leaves and fern fronds to raise themselves above the leaf litter.

In Cameroon a western pygmy chameleon picks its way along a dead leaf whose colors provide perfect camouflage.

Breeding

Unlike many of the *Chamaeleo* species, there is no dramatic color change in western pygmy chameleons during courtship. The males' coloration becomes paler, and mated females exhibit some red mottling. Four to six weeks after a successful mating the female lays two (sometimes three or four) eggs among the leaf litter on the forest floor. The decomposition of leaves provides a stable temperature and constant humidity levels, making it an ideal environment for incubation. The eggs, which are laid at a relatively advanced stage, hatch about six to eight weeks later.

Although the habitat of the western pygmy chameleon is seasonal, the only dry period is between June and August, so the chameleons usually breed for most of the year.

Warning Vibrations

When under stress, including being held in the mouth of a predator or in human hands, the western pygmy chameleon is capable of emitting a number of short vibrations that make no sound. Each vibration lasts for about one second and is repeated until the threat goes away.

The chameleon appears to make the vibrations by exhaling small amounts of air. It is thought that this behavior is defensive and is intended to startle the predator. If it is holding the chameleon in its jaws at the time, it will drop it, and the chameleon can escape.

Iguanas

C urrent understanding is that there are 892 species of iguanas. Some scientists believe that they should be divided into smaller units and that each unit should be regarded as a separate family. Others consider them to be subfamilies, which is how they are treated here.

The iguanids have an interesting distribution in South, Central, and North America and in Madagascar. Their distribution is similar to that of the boas and is evidence of continental drift. About 100 million years ago South America, Africa, and Madagascar formed a large southern landmass called Gondwanaland. When Gondwanaland broke apart, iguanas were trapped on

⬆ ➡ *Representative iguanids. The Cuban brown anole,* Anolis sagrei, *subfamily Polychrotinae(1); the rhinoceros iguana,* Cyclura cychlura, *subfamily Iguaninae (2); the fringe-toed lizard,* Uma notata, *subfamily Phrynosomatinae (3).*

Common name Iguanas **Family** Iguanidae

Family Iguanidae
Although there is some dispute over the classification of iguanas, they are usually divided into eight subfamilies (some of which are considered full families by some authorities) and about 892 species iin 44 genera:

Subfamily Corytophaninae—3 genera, 9 species of medium-sized basilisks and related species from Central and South America, including the plumed basilisk, *Basiliscus plumifrons*

Subfamily Crotaphytinae—2 genera, 10 species of medium-sized collared and leopard lizards from North America, including *Crotaphytus collaris*

Subfamily Hoplocercinae—3 genera, 10 species from Central and South America

Subfamily Iguaninae—8 genera, 36 species of large iguanas from Central and South America, incorporating the Galápagos Islands, Cuba, and the West Indies; species include the green iguana, *Iguana iguana*, the marine iguana, *Amblyrhynchus cristatus*, and the Galápagos land iguana, *Conolophus subcristatus*

Subfamily Oplurinae—2 genera, 7 species of Madagascan iguanas, including the Madagascar collared lizard, *Oplurus cuvieri*

Subfamily Phrynosomatinae—9 genera, about 124 species of horned lizards, fence lizards, and side-blotched lizards from North and Central America, including the side-blotched lizard, *Uta stansburiana*, the coast horned lizard, *Phrynosoma coronatum*, and the western fence lizard, *Sceloporus occidentalis*

Subfamily Polychrotinae—8 genera, 394 species of anoles and relatives from North, Central, and South America (especially the Caribbean region), including the green anole, *Anolis carolinensis*

Subfamily Tropidurinae—9 genera, 302 species of lava lizards and relatives from South America, Galápagos, and the West Indies, including the Galápagos lava lizards, *Microlophus* sp.

---

each of the newly formed, smaller landmasses. They died out in Africa and were replaced by members of a similar family, the Agamidae, which are their ecological counterparts. However, on Madagascar they survived in the form of two genera: *Oplurus* (with six species) and *Chalarodon* (with just one species, the four-eyed lizard, *C. madagascarensis*). Other groups spread west by a process known as rafting. Ancestral stocks from South or Central America, perhaps similar to the spiny-tailed iguanas that live there today, were swept out to sea and drifted on the ocean currents. Nearly all of them would have died long before they reached land, but a lucky few made it to pastures new—the Galápagos Islands—where three large species and seven small species live. Remarkably, others continued their voyage as far as the Fijian Islands and Tonga, where there are two large and colorful species, *Brachylophus fasciatus* and *B. vitiensis*. Others colonized several Caribbean islands; they included a few large species such as the rhinoceros iguanas, *Cyclura* species, and a multitude of small, agile species belonging to the genus *Anolis* and related genera.

Once the land connection between South and North America was made, iguanids spread northward along the isthmus of Panama and into Mexico and the United States, where small iguanids in the subfamily Phrynosomatinae (horned lizards and side-blotched

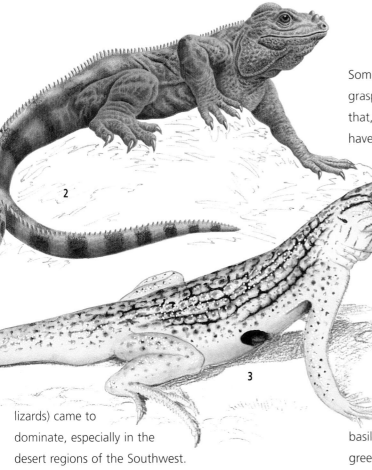

2

3

Some have the ability to discard part of their tail if it is grasped, a trick known as caudal autotomy. Having said that, three species of *Uracentron* from South America have thick, heavily armored tails that cannot be autotomized. These lizards live in forest canopies and sleep in tree holes, and they can use their tails to block out predators from the openings.

Sexual dimorphism is widespread across the family. Males are often larger than females, sometimes massively so. For example, in the marine iguanas, *Amblyrhynchus cristatus* from the Galápagos Islands, males can weigh up to four times more than females. Males are often more likely to have crests on their backs and heads; or if both sexes have them, those of the males are larger. In basilisks only males have crests on their heads, while in green iguanas, for example, females have reduced crests.

lizards) came to dominate, especially in the desert regions of the Southwest.

Form and Function

It is difficult to define a "typical" iguanid. We are inclined to think of the large, spectacular species such as the green iguana, *Iguana iguana*, the Galápagos land iguana, *Conolophus subcristatus*, and the marine iguana, *Amblyrhynchus cristatus*, with stocky bodies and large, saw-tooth crests along their backs. In fact, they make up just a tiny minority of iguanids.

Most are quite small with slender bodies without crests or other ornamentation. Most have relatively large, keeled scales, but some have small, granular ones. The members of the family must value their limbs, since there is no tendency for them to become small or disappear altogether as in many other families—many iguanids are long legged and very agile. Fast-running species can lift their front feet off the ground as they gather speed and run on the hind legs only (known as bipedal locomotion). The plumed basilisk, *Basiliscus plumifrons* from Central America, can even run across water, a talent that has locally earned it the name "Jesus Christ lizard."

Iguanids typically have long tails and often use them for counterbalance, curling them up in the air as they run.

Color and Communication

Nearly all iguanas communicate visually, and males often have elaborate display routines that can include head bobbing, pushups, or the lowering of dewlaps. To this end, some male iguanids are very colorful, and many have bright patches to enhance their displays: The anoles have brightly colored dewlaps, for example, that act as "flags" when they flick them up and down. Female *Anolis* species often have dewlaps too, but those of males are larger and more showy. This probably reflects the fact that females can be territorial in some species but not as aggressively so as males. Dominant male collared lizards, *Crotaphytus collaris*, Peruvian swifts, *Liolaemus* species, and lava lizards, *Microlophis* species (to name just a few), often glow with color during the breeding season, while subordinate males, females, and juveniles are much duller by comparison.

Male iguanids can increase their visibility further by standing stiff legged and bobbing up and down to attract attention, often displaying bright patches of color that are hidden when they are at rest. Some of them pose on prominent rocks or tree stumps where they can be seen many yards away, a habit that gives the fence lizards their common name. Males of the species have bright patches on their throats and chests, which are only visible when they raise their bodies off the ground. They become cryptic (disguised) when at rest to avoid attracting the attention of predators.

However, the markings on some species are designed to attract the attention of predators. Several species, such as the zebra-tailed lizard, *Callisaurus draconoides*, the Texas earless lizard, *Holbrookia texanus*, and the fringe-toed lizards, *Uma* species, have black bands on the underside of their tails, which are otherwise white. They raise their tails and wave them from side to side when they see a predator, which is thought to be a signal telling the predator that it has been spotted. It is intended to persuade the predator that the lizard is not worth stalking and, at the same time, saves the lizard from using energy in running away.

Coloration can also send other signals. Females of several species develop orange areas on their flanks when they are carrying eggs. The color tells males that they have already mated and avoids both male and female wasting time and energy in courtship and rebuff.

General Behavior

The great majority of iguanids are diurnal. They typically bask in exposed places to gain body heat before going off to forage for food or look for a mate. Some live in the deep shade of forest floors and in the understory, however, and experiments have shown that those species operate below their preferred body temperatures for much of the time.

A few are unusual. The *Uracentron* species live high up in the forest canopy and are therefore rarely seen. They seem to exist in colonies containing a single dominant male, a number of smaller, subordinate males, and females and juveniles of varying ages. They move through the canopy in large groups. Another atypical species is *Uranoscodon superciliosus* from the Amazon Basin in Brazil and neighboring countries. It lives at the water's edge along rivercourses, moving out into the forest when the rivers flood. It forages among the flotsam

and jetsam in search of living and dead invertebrates. In the humid environment algae grows on its scales, which enhances its camouflage. In fact, it relies so heavily on camouflage that it rarely moves, even when approached closely. It is therefore known locally as the "blind lizard," implying that it is unaware of danger.

The marine iguana, *Amblyrhynchus cristatus*, is unique not just among iguanas but among lizards as a whole because it feeds in the sea. However, there are other iguanids that live along the shore, feeding on small isopods known as slaters. Like the marine iguana, these species (the side-blotched lizards in the genus *Uta*) gather excess salt in salt glands situated near their nostrils.

At the other extreme some iguanids live in the most arid deserts. The fringe-toed lizards, for example, live among dunes in the American Southwest. As their name suggests, they have long, pointed scales around the edges of their toes, forming a fringe that helps them run across loose, windblown sand. They have additional adaptations in the form of a countersunk lower jaw and flaps over their ear openings that prevent sand from entering their ears and mouth when burrowing. They also have extremely sensitive hearing and typically stand on the surface of the sand with their head cocked to one side listening for sounds of insects moving beneath the surface. Then they dive headfirst into the sand to catch them. When chased by predators, they run rapidly across the surface, often lifting their front feet from the ground before plunging into the sand.

Diet and Feeding

Among them the iguanas consume just about the whole range of potential food. The larger species, such as the desert iguana, *Dipsosaurus dorsalis*, the rhinoceros iguanas, *Cyclura* species, and the chuckwallas, *Sauromalus* species, are completely herbivorous. They often feed on sparse desert vegetation, including cactus leaves and fruit and desert flowers. By contrast, the

⊙ **Sceloporus malachiticus** *is known as the green spiny lizard. It is found at higher altitudes in Central America. Some members of the genus give birth to live young and are among the few iguanids to do so.*

marine iguana eats only seaweed. Medium-sized species such as the collared lizards, *Crotaphrytus* species, are voracious predators. They eat large insects and spiders, and they are especially fond of smaller lizards.

Most small iguanids are insectivores, eating a wide variety of small prey. The horned lizards, *Phrynosoma* species from the American Southwest and Mexico, feed almost exclusively on ants and eat huge quantities at a single sitting.

Foraging behavior also varies. The herbivorous species forage actively, most small and medium-sized species feed opportunistically, while others adopt a "sit-and-wait" technique. Horned lizards station themselves alongside ant trails, picking off the ants as they pass by.

Habitat

Iguanids have moved into almost every available habitat within the region they occupy. Many North American species live in deserts, adapting well to intense heat and scarce food. They are fast, agile hunters, seizing every opportunity to chase down and capture small prey or developing special techniques for exploiting prey animals that tend to gather in one place.

Others exist on seemingly unpalatable cactus pads, twigs, and dried-up vegetation, eating constantly in order to accumulate what little nourishment they can. Iguanas from dry habitats often live in burrows, or they can be "sand swimmers," paralleling species in other families, such as the sandfish, *Scinus scinus* (Scincidae), and the wedge- and shovel-snouted lizards from the Namib Desert (in the family Lacertidae).

Iguanids have successfully colonized many islands, and are the dominant lizard family over most of the West Indies, on the many small islands in the Gulf of California, and on the Galápagos Islands. Some species exploit the seashore as a source of vegetable or animal food, while others hang around seabird colonies feeding on spilled fish or the flies that are attracted to such places.

On many small islands that would otherwise be barren, seabirds provide the only ecological input by fishing surrounding waters and returning to shore with their harvest. Species such as the side-blotched lizards,

Uta species, have been quick to exploit the service provided by the seabirds.

Tropical forests are the habitats that are the richest in species, especially of anoles and related iguanids. In any given area it is not unusual to find three or four separate species "sharing" the resources by occupying slightly different microhabitats: There may be a terrestrial, an arboreal, and a shrub-dwelling species, for example, or they may vary in size and therefore prefer different prey. They may even prey on each other.

⬆ *In North America a clutch of eggs laid by a northern fence lizard,* Sceloporus undulatus hyacinthinus, *begins to hatch out. The eggs are laid in loose soil or sand and take from 60 to 80 days to incubate.*

⬅ *A spiny-tailed lizard,* Uracentron azureum, *from French Guiana. Like other members of its genus, it has a heavily armored tail that cannot be broken off.*

cool montane areas to give birth, a good example being Yarrow's spiny lizard, *Sceloporus jarrovi*. However, other live-bearers, such as the crevice spiny lizard, *S. poinsettii*, and the Central American green spiny lizard, *S. malachiticus*, live in warmer habitats.

Many iguanids have complex breeding systems in which a single dominant male controls territory containing several adult females (and sometimes also younger, subordinate males and juveniles). Opportunities for research into lizard behavior are good, especially where colonies can be observed easily in habitats such as deserts and open scrub, and some interesting studies have resulted in recent years.

The competition for good territory and the females it contains leads to a selective pressure that favors large, more powerful, and more colorful males. Males of some species operate a "lek" type of system more commonly associated with birds, in which males congregate in well-defined areas and battle for the right to mate with nearby females. Alternative strategies have also evolved in which smaller and less assertive males "steal" matings using a variety of "dirty tricks" to gain access to the females.

Breeding

Most iguanids are egg layers, but a few give birth to live young. Both types can be present even within the same genus, as in the horned lizards, *Phrynosoma*, and the South American swifts, *Liolaemus*. In both cases there is a correlation with habitat—species from warm lowlands tend to lay eggs, while those from higher, cooler altitudes give birth. Live-bearing seems to have evolved several times within the spiny lizards, *Sceloporus*. Within the genus there is also a tendency for those species living in

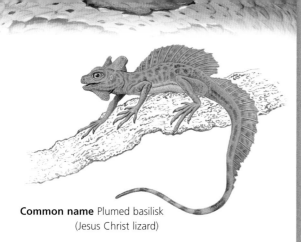

Common name Plumed basilisk
(Jesus Christ lizard)

Scientific name *Basiliscus plumifrons*

Subfamily Corytophaninae

Family Iguanidae

Suborder Sauria

Order Squamata

Size Males to 36 inches (91 cm); females to 20
inches (51 cm), of which the tail can account
for three-quarters

Key features Adults green with black bars on the tail
and lighter green or white spots on the
flanks; both sexes have a crest on their head
(the male's has two lobes); male also has
separate crests on the back and tail; body
and tail flattened from side to side; front legs
and tail very long; juveniles are spidery in
appearance with long, thin legs

Habits Arboreal or semiarboreal; diurnal

Breeding Egg layer that breeds throughout the year;
female lays 4–17 eggs that hatch after about
65 days

Diet Small vertebrates, invertebrates, and plant
material

Habitat Forests (usually in the vicinity of water)

Distribution Central America (eastern Honduras to
southwestern Costa Rica)

Status Common in suitable habitat

Similar species There are other basilisks in the region,
but *B. plumifrons* is the only bright green
one; other green iguanids of similar size
lack crests

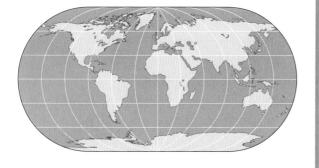

Plumed Basilisk
Basiliscus plumifrons

*The colorful plumed basilisk lives in the forests of
Central America. It is never far from water, which
often provides it with an escape route when
faced with danger.*

BASILISKS HAVE AN AMAZING ability to run across the
surface of still water, a habit that has given
them the alternative common name of Jesus
Christ lizard. Their long toes have a fringe of
rectangular, projecting scales that can rest on
the surface film without breaking through, as
long as the basilisk keeps moving. Once they
get going, they lift the front of their body up,
hold their front legs against their chest, and run
on their long hinds legs, curving their tail up in
an arc to act as a counterbalance. Small
individuals do not even need to move very fast
to remain on the surface and often seem to
move in slow motion at first before accelerating
across a patch of open water, leaving a twin
trail of ripples. Sometimes a small group will
break cover and run off together in formation.
They are also good swimmers and can swim
underwater for long distances.

Daytime Foragers

Basilisks usually occur in dense vegetation along
streams and rivers, and often sleep on branches
overhanging water. If they are disturbed by a
predator, they are quick to drop into the water
and may swim to the bottom. During the day
they forage among the vegetation, eating more
or less anything they find. Juveniles are almost
entirely insectivorous; but as they grow, their
diet becomes more varied, and they will also
take leaves, fruit, and berries. Large adults
sometimes tackle crustaceans such as shrimp
and crabs, and have even been known to eat
snakes and sleeping bats.

Like many tropical lizards, they breed
throughout the year, although most activity
takes place during the rainy season (May to
September in Costa Rica, for instance). The

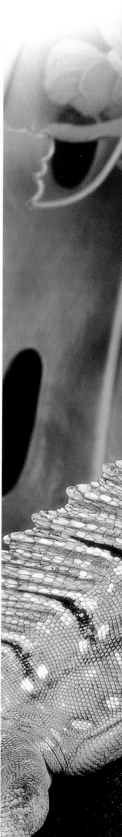

⊕ *The plumed basilisk,* Basiliscus plumifrons, *is one of the fastest lizards, able to run at speeds in excess of 6.5 feet (2 m) per second. It is also the most colorful species in the genus, the others being dull brown in color.*

female lays four to 17 eggs in a short nest chamber that the lizards excavate themselves. The eggs take about 65 days to hatch. The babies are dull in color and show no signs of the crests, which develop later as low ridges of skin that gradually increase in size. The crests on the head are fleshy and often become torn and somewhat ragged, while those on the back and tail of males are supported by elongated, bony spines projecting up from the vertebrae.

The Relatives

There are four species of basilisk altogether, ranging from Mexico to Ecuador and western Venezuela. All have crests, but only the plumed basilisk is bright green in color. They favor waterside habitats, except for the striped basilisk, *B. vittatus*, which can be found far from water in open places, including disturbed habitats such as pastures and coconut plantations. Like *B. plumifrons,* it is capable of walking on two legs (bipedal locomotion) across water if the need arises.

Mythological Creature

The basilisk is an ancient mythological beast with the legs and head of a rooster, the body, tail, and tongue of a snake, and the wings of a bat. The similarities to the basilisk lizard, therefore, are the crest (which is like the comb of a rooster), the long, snakelike tail, and the bright, staring eyes. The basilisk from mythology could kill everything it encountered with its stare, and the only defense against it was to hold up a mirror, whereupon its own reflection would frighten it to death.

The English playwright William Shakespeare often used herpetological metaphors, including one about a basilisk. In *Richard III* (Act I, Scene 2) Lady Anne responds to Richard's compliment about her eyes, "Would they were basilisk's, to strike thee dead!" It seems there is just no pleasing some folk!

Common name Collared lizard

Scientific name *Crotaphytus collaris*

Subfamily Crotaphytinae

Family Iguanidae

Suborder Sauria

Order Squamata

Size To 10 in (25cm); males are larger than females

Key features Head massive; 2 black rings around the neck; tail long and cylindrical; hind limbs long; body covered in small scales, giving the skin a silky texture; body color varies among populations and with the season but is typically green in males, dull green, brown, or yellowish in females, all with light spots loosely arranged into transverse lines; juveniles have distinct banding across the back that gradually fades as the animal grows

Habits Diurnal and heat loving; lives on the ground and rarely climbs, except among boulders

Breeding Egg layer with more than one clutch each year; female lays 1–13 eggs that hatch after about 45 days

Diet Large invertebrates and smaller lizards; also some vegetable material, including leaves and flowers

Habitat Hot, rocky hillsides with sparse vegetation

Distribution Western United States in desert regions

Status Common

Similar species There are other collared lizards, but their ranges do not overlap; the leopard lizards, *Gambelia*, are their only other close relatives

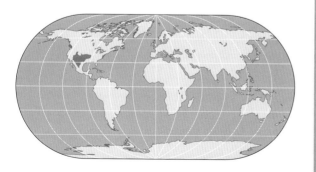

Collared Lizard

Crotaphytus collaris

Collared lizards are noted for running upright on their hind legs, making them look like miniature Tyrannosaurus rex. *They are powerful hunters and have an unusual way of waving their tail, like a cat, before grabbing at prey.*

THERE ARE EIGHT SPECIES OF COLLARED LIZARDS and three species of leopard lizards. Together they make up the subfamily Crotaphytinae, which is sometimes regarded as a full family, the Crotaphytidae. All collared lizards are broadly similar in size and shape, and all have two black collars separated by a white or light-colored one, although their general coloration varies. For instance, *C. vestigium* from Baja California and California, is rich chocolate-brown with pure white spots and bands fading to dull orange or green on its flanks. The spectacular Dickerson's collared lizard, *C. dickersonae*, is sometimes regarded as a subspecies of *C. collaris*. The males are deep blue in color.

The other half of the family, the leopard lizards, consists of three species with slightly more slender heads and bodies than the collared lizards. They prefer open habitat, such as sand and gravel flats with sparse vegetation, for example, creosote bush scrub. They shelter in burrows at night. They are pale buff or sandy brown in color and often wait for prey at the base of a small bush, where the dappled shadow helps disguise their outline. When approached by predators, leopard lizards often flatten themselves to the surface and rely on their pale camouflage colors to escape notice.

Fearless Terrorists

Collared lizards are powerful hunters—they are likely to terrorize smaller lizards from the region. They chase them down and crush them in their powerful jaws before swallowing them whole. Collared lizards also eat large invertebrates such as grasshoppers and beetles. They dominate south-facing rocky ridges and

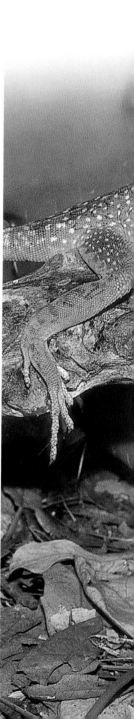

SEE ALSO Agamas and Dragon Lizards **44**:32; Chameleons **44**:56; Iguanas **44**:80

Collared lizards exhibit sexual dimorphism, as seen in this pair of Crotaphytus collaris from Texas. The male (left) is predominantly green, while the female (right) is yellowish brown in color. Males are also larger than females.

hillsides by taking up positions on prominent boulders. From there they can survey the large area over which they hunt. Males are especially territorial. They stand up on stiff limbs and bob their body up and down if another collared lizard approaches. They will even display to humans, standing their ground until the last minute. Then they dash off, sometimes lifting the front part of their body off the ground and taking huge strides with their hind legs. At the same time, they raise their tail as a counterweight. Their aggressive behavior has persuaded local people, especially in Mexico, that collared lizards are venomous.

Breeding Coloration

Collared lizards come into breeding condition in the spring, often in late March or early April after several

months in hibernation. At that time of year the male's colors really glow once he has warmed up by basking on the hottest exposed rocks. Dominant males mate with all the females living within their territory. Once females have mated and their eggs begin to develop, they too undergo a color change. Large patches of bright orange appear on their flanks and the sides of their neck, showing that they are full of eggs (this is known as "gravid coloration"). The color probably indicates to the male that she is not receptive to more mating attempts. This prevents further attempts at courtship and saves both of them time and energy.

Gravid coloration is not unique to collared lizards: It is present in many other iguanids and in some agamid lizards and chameleons. The exact color varies from species to species, but it is invariably bright, distinctive, and easily visible from a distance. Females lay one to 13 eggs, which they bury, and which hatch after about 45 days. Each female lays two or more clutches throughout the summer provided she can find enough food to replenish her reserves. The hatchlings, the last of which emerges in late summer or early fall, lack the bright colors of adults and are mostly brown with a black collar.

Common name Marine iguana

Scientific name *Amblyrhynchus cristatus*

Subfamily Iguaninae

Family Iguanidae

Suborder Sauria

Order Squamata

Size From 30 in (75 cm) to 4.1 ft (1.3 m)

Key features Heavy bodied with muscular limbs and a powerful tail; a crest of elongated, toothlike scales runs along the center of the back and tail; top of the head covered with horny, conical scales of varying sizes; color usually gray, although some subspecies are more colorful with patches of red or turquoise

Habits Diurnal, basking by day on rocks and entering the sea to feed

Breeding Egg layer; female lays 1–6 eggs in tunnels on shore; eggs hatch after about 95 days

Diet Marine algae (seaweed)

Habitat Rocky seashores

Distribution Galápagos Islands

Status Protected under national legislation but possibly at risk in the long term from human pressures

Similar species The marine iguana is unmistakable; the only other iguanas on the islands are the Galápagos land iguanas, *Conolophus subcristatus*, and the much smaller lava lizards, *Microlophus* sp.

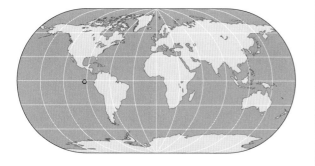

Marine Iguana

Amblyrhynchus cristatus

Marine iguanas are unique. They are the only seagoing lizards and the only lizards that feed on seaweed—a lifestyle that has resulted in many special adaptations.

AFTER VISITING THE GALÁPAGOS ISLANDS, the English naturalist Charles Darwin wrote, "The rocks on the coast are abounded with great black lizards between three and four feet long; it is a hideous-looking creature, of a dirty black colour, stupid and sluggish in its movements." We have no idea what they thought of him!

The Galápagos Islands straddle the equator and are about 600 miles (1,550 km) off the coast of Ecuador. The ocean there is very cold, but the Humboldt Current drives up the west coast of South America and brings with it the waters of the Antarctic, rich in nutrients and fish. Much of the land, on the other hand, is barren, formed by lava that resulted from the volcanic eruptions to which the Galápagos owe their existence.

Marine iguanas arrived on the Galápagos from South or Central America many thousands of generations ago and adapted to an environment in which food was readily available in the sea but not on the land. Their ancestors would have been one of the larger iguanas, possibly something like the spiny-tailed iguanas, *Ctenosaura*, that live on the mainland today. A few individuals (or a single gravid female) were swept out to sea on a raft of vegetation and drifted west until they washed up on one of the islands. Later they spread to all the larger islands as well as many smaller islets in the archipelago. Some populations, particularly on far-flung islands, evolved distinct sizes and coloration, and scientists recognize seven separate races, or subspecies.

Diving and Feeding

The iguanas' most remarkable talent is for diving, which is how they find the seaweed on which they feed. Although a typical dive lasts

⬇ *Marine iguanas are just as at home beneath the water as on land. Large adults can graze among rocks in shallows for up to an hour.*

only for a few minutes, large iguanas can stay underwater for up to an hour and reach depths of 40 feet (12 m). The amount of time they can spend in the water is limited by temperature. The water is only a few degrees above freezing; being ectotherms, the iguanas lose mobility if their body temperature falls too low. Larger individuals (mostly males) can store heat in the core of their bodies, but females, young males, and juveniles get cold quickly. As a result, there are two different groups: divers and nondivers.

The feeding patterns of large males depend on temperature. They bask on the lava rocks during the morning until their core body temperature has reached the preferred level—about 100 to 104°F (38–40°C). Then they make their way down to the water regardless of the state of the tide and swim several hundred yards out to sea before diving down to the beds of sea lettuce that grow below the low-tide mark. Between dives they can crawl out onto

emergent reefs or return to the shore to bask and top up their temperature. They swim by holding their limbs close to their body and swinging their tail from side to side to propel them through the waves and surf.

By late afternoon their body temperature is falling to the point where they can hardly

⊖ *On the Galápagos Islands marine iguanas bask to raise their body temperature before plunging into the cold sea to feed.*

Island Races

There is little or no gene exchange between the iguana populations on different islands because they are not able to swim large distances. Many of the more remote islands were probably only colonized once many thousands of years ago, perhaps by a handful of waifs after storms in the region. Other islands (those that are closer to their neighbors) may have had several "invasions." Scientists have recognized some of the differences and have divided the marine iguana into seven races, or subspecies. The first three subspecies, which appear to be closely related, come from the westernmost islands where the seas are richer. Consequently, they grow slightly larger than the other subspecies.

> *Amblyrhynchus cristatus cristatus*—large, dark gray form from Fernandina Island
>
> *A. c. albemarlensis*—largest form, also gray, from Isabela
>
> *A. c. hassi*—large gray form from Santa Cruz
>
> *A. c. mertensi*—medium form from Santiago and San Cristóbal
>
> *A. c. nanus*—very small, black in color, from the remote northern island of Genovesa
>
> *A. c. sielmanni*—medium-sized form from Pinta
>
> *A. c. venustissimus*—a large, spectacular form from Española with deep red patches on its body

move, so they make their way back to shore and crawl slowly up the beach and rocks until they reach a place where they will spend the night. They prefer the company of hundreds of other large iguanas and form great heaps that help limit heat loss from their bodies.

Females and smaller males have a completely different routine. They do not dive but feed on the algae that is exposed at low tide. Females and subadult males may have to swim across short channels of water to reach it, but juveniles never take to the water. They lose heat too quickly and are vulnerable to predation in open water. An average-sized adult can survive on about 1 ounce (28 g) of algae each day partly because its metabolism is slow but also because red and green seaweeds are very nutritious. Brown algae, however, is poor in nutrients, and the iguanas refuse it unless they are desperate.

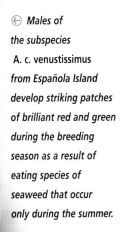

① Head-butting matches between rival males can last for hours or even days. This pair of males belongs to the subspecies A. c. mertensi from Santiago Island.

⟵ Males of the subspecies A. c. venustissimus from Española Island develop striking patches of brilliant red and green during the breeding season as a result of eating species of seaweed that occur only during the summer.

The iguanas' snouts are very short, and their mouths are bordered by tough scales so that they can crop the algae closely. Feeding iguanas are often pounded by large waves and seem as though they must be washed off the rocks and out to sea. However, they cling to the lava with very long claws like grappling hooks and remain in the same position until the surf subsides before continuing to graze.

Because they spend so much time in the sea and because they eat seaweed, marine iguanas accumulate a lot of excess salt in their system. To counteract this, they have salt glands just above their nostrils where the excess salt accumulates. While they bask, they eliminate it by snorting fine sprays of concentrated salt water from their nostrils at regular intervals.

Breeding

Mating takes place from November through to January or February but varies a little from one island to another. The large males defend territories containing many females; at this time the males become more colorful, often reddish or greenish depending on locality. They posture with much head bobbing and strutting. Rivals are chased away. If they persist, a fight breaks out. The head butting and shoving can last for several hours with short breaks between bouts. When two males are well matched, the bouts can continue on successive days with both males becoming bruised and bloody.

During mating the male mounts the female and grasps her neck in his jaws while he forces the rear part of his body under hers so that copulation can take place. Mating can last for several minutes. Small males, however, can "steal" matings lasting only a few seconds; to increase their chances of fertilizing the female, they transfer sperm into their hemipenal sacs before mating. Males probably take about 10 years to reach a dominant position in the colony, and each male controls a territory that can contain several dozen females.

A few weeks after mating, females look for suitable egg-laying sites. They are often several hundred yards back from the shore in sand or shingle. The eggs, numbering one to six, are laid at the end of a short tunnel and then covered over. Good sites are in short supply, and females often stay near their eggs to chase away other gravid females that may dig up the nest while excavating a tunnel of their own. During this time they look emaciated and in poor shape.

The eggs hatch after about 95 days, and the young iguanas dig their way out of the ground and make their way to the shore. They are very vulnerable to predation, especially by Galápagos hawks, snakes, and gulls. Hatchlings and juveniles live a secretive life hidden in crevices in the lava and only emerge for short periods to feed. They never go to sea; instead, they graze on algae in the spray zone. Nor do they bask, but close contact with the dark lava causes heat to transfer to their bodies.

Future Prospects

Marine iguanas have few predators once they are adult. Juveniles are eaten by the few snakes on the islands and by birds of prey. Gulls take a few of the hatchlings. On many islands humans have introduced feral populations of rats, cats, dogs, and pigs, which destroy nests and eat hatchlings. Up to 60 percent of juveniles may die during their first year.

Tourism may have some negative effects because of increased disturbance and pollution. On balance, however, it is probably beneficial, because it brings much-needed income to the islands and in particular to the Galápagos

National Park, which accounts for nearly all the area covered by the archipelago. Programs to eliminate feral goats and other pest species are funded by tourist dollars.

Marine iguanas are not found anywhere else in the world. They must be considered vulnerable to any serious environmental disaster along the lines of the oil tanker that sank off the islands a few years ago. Such events could wipe out whole populations. In addition, the human population of the Galápagos has swollen from 4,000 to 12,000 at the end of the 20th century, mainly through migrants from the mainland who are attracted by work in the tourism and fishing industries. Unless the influx of people is carefully managed, it is bound to put pressure on the environment.

⊖ *Marine iguanas are protected by national legislation, but they are vulnerable to marine pollution and the effects of human development.*

El Niño

The El Niño phenomenon has serious implications for the marine iguanas. During El Niño years the warm waters of the western Pacific push farther east than usual and prevent the cold, rich waters of the Humboldt Current from welling up to the surface. The result is more cloud and heavier rainfall in the Galápagos, killing much of the algae on which the iguanas feed. Up to 90 percent of the lizards may die during those years.

El Niño years used to occur roughly every seven years; but for reasons that are not fully understood, they now occur more often—sometimes every second year—and the frequency prevents populations from recovering. The hundreds of iguanas that used to be seen basking on Punta Espinosa on Fernandina, for instance, may soon be a thing of the past. Individual iguanas in good condition may be able to draw on stored food reserves, and there is evidence that they may also be able to shrink themselves by up to 2 percent to limit the damage.

The effects of El Niño are also significant for the other animals for which the Galápagos Islands are famous. The seabirds, including endemic gulls, boobies, albatrosses, and frigate birds, all rely on fish for their food, and the warmer water drives away fish stocks. Many seabirds fail to raise a family during El Niño years.

Common name Galápagos land iguana

Scientific name *Conolophus subcristatus*

Subfamily Iguaninae

Family Iguanidae

Suborder Sauria

Order Squamata

Size To 39 in (100 cm)

Key features Heavy bodied and ponderous with pointed scales covering the head; a low crest of small, tooth-shaped scales runs along the ridge of the back and onto the tail; limbs short, thick, and powerful; toes end in long claws used for digging burrows; color variable with head, limbs, and flanks ranging from uniform dark brown to a pattern of bright golden yellow; back darker

Habits Diurnal; terrestrial but sometimes climbs into shrubs in search of food

Breeding Egg layer; female lays up to 25 eggs

Diet Vegetation, especially the pads and fruits of prickly pear cacti, *Opuntia* sp.

Habitat Hot, dry, rocky islands

Distribution Galápagos Islands; at present only found on Santa Cruz, Isabela, Fernandina, Plaza Sur, North Seymour, and Baltra

Status Secure on some islands, dwindling on others; extinct from many islands where it once lived

Similar species The pale land iguana, *Conolophus pallidus*, is similar but light grayish brown in color and restricted to a single island, Santa Fé

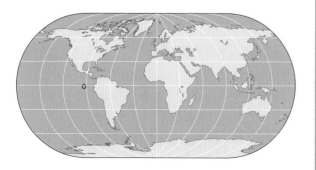

Galápagos Land Iguana

Conolophus subcristatus

The great big, lumbering land iguanas are the terrestrial equivalents of the marine iguanas with which they share their isolated Pacific archipelago.

LAND IGUANAS LEAD SEDENTARY LIVES, crawling out of their burrows in the morning to bask and warm up their considerable body mass. Then they may go in search of food, although a common strategy is to sit under a prickly pear cactus bush and wait for the wind to blow down a pad, or better still, a ripe fruit. Clearly, this can take some time—often several days—and the iguana may nibble at low ground vegetation while waiting for the main course to arrive. Impatient iguanas sometimes clamber into cactus bushes or other shrubs in search of food.

On islands where the food supply is plentiful, such as Plaza Sur, iguanas occur in high densities and are easily seen by visitors. Elsewhere, for example, on parts of Isabela, the grazing of introduced goats has drastically reduced the iguanas' food supply, and their numbers are dwindling. Once covered in iguana burrows, the island of Santiago now has no iguanas due to human disturbance or to the animals that have been introduced by humans.

Male land iguanas are highly territorial at all times but especially during the breeding season. If others approach them, they nod their head vigorously and do not hesitate to fight. Males mate with any females that enter their territory.

Heroic Females

Females lay up to 25 eggs in burrows they dig for themselves. They too can be territorial at this time to keep newly arrived females from digging up their nests. On the island of Fernandina, which is especially rocky, females make a heroic journey of several miles up the sides of a dormant volcano and down into the

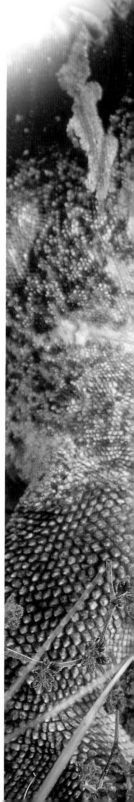

crater to lay their eggs. The small hatchlings have to climb the crater wall and make their way back to the feeding grounds, running the gauntlet of Galápagos hawks as they go.

Juveniles are rarely seen here or on other islands, because they keep under cover to avoid predation. They eat invertebrates such as beetles and grasshoppers while young and gradually switch to a vegetarian diet as they grow. Adults will eat carrion if the opportunity arises, however. Few juveniles survive to reach adult size, but those that do are reasonably safe and can live to 60 years old.

A slightly different land iguana lives on the island of Santa Fé and nowhere else. It is a paler, uniformly dull-brown species, *Conolophus pallidus*. It is similar to the more widespread species apart from its coloration and a slightly higher dorsal crest. A third type is sometimes seen, especially on Plaza Sur. It is a hybrid between the marine iguana, *Amblyrhynchus cristatus*, and the land iguana. It seems to behave like a land iguana, eating cactus and other plants and never entering the water, but its coloration is dark, like the marine iguana. The implication is that both species are closely related despite the obvious difference in their habitat preferences.

⊕ **With their long tails, clawed feet, scaly skin, and spiny crests the Galápagos land iguanas resemble mythical dragons.**

Repatriated Iguanas

The situation on North Seymour is interesting from a conservation viewpoint. When the American adventurer William Hearst visited the island in the 1930s, he found there were no iguanas at all (and probably never had been). Just across the water on Baltra, however, there was a healthy iguana population. Hearst decided to give nature a helping hand: He caught some of the Baltra animals and let them go on Seymour. These days his actions would be frowned on, but luckily it turned out well for the iguanas. The original Baltra population was exterminated when an American airbase was built on the island during World War II. The population on Seymour did not thrive exactly, but there were enough left to reintroduce some of them back onto Baltra.

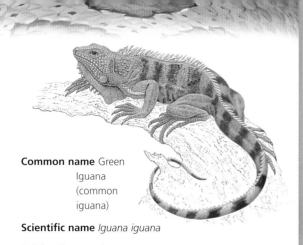

Common name Green Iguana (common iguana)

Scientific name *Iguana iguana*

Subfamily Iguaninae

Family Iguanidae

Suborder Sauria

Order Squamata

Size Males to 6.6 ft (2 m), females to 4.8 ft (1.4 m)

Key features Very large green or greenish lizards; adults have crest of tooth-shaped scales along the back and the first third of the tail; tail has broad, dark bands around it; limbs long; each toe is also long and has claws for grasping; large males develop a flap of skin (dewlap) under the chin (in females it is smaller); a single, very large smooth scale present on each side of the head below the eardrum in both males and females

Habits Arboreal; diurnal

Breeding Egg layers with large clutches of 9–71 eggs; eggs hatch after 65–115 days

Diet Mostly vegetation, especially leaves

Habitat Forests, especially rain forests but also dry deciduous forests in some places

Distribution Central and South America (northwestern Mexico in the north to Ecuador, northern Bolivia, Paraguay, and southern Brazil to the south); also on some West Indian islands and introduced to Florida

Status Common in places but under pressure from humans in others

Similar species The closely related *Iguana delicatissima* from the Lesser Antilles (West Indies)

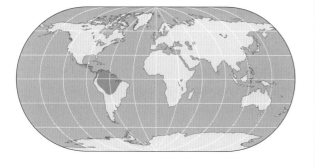

Green Iguana

Iguana iguana

The green iguana is an instantly recognizable lizard from Central and South America. It is a dinosaurlike lizard of impressive proportions that lives in the highest tree canopies.

Although the green iguana is not tied to the water to the same extent as some other iguanids, such as the plumed basilisk, *Basiliscus plumifrons*, it is most often seen along the edges of rivers. Since it is easier to see into the tops of tall trees that are isolated at the edge of rivers than those that are surrounded by other trees, it is possible that green iguanas are everywhere in the forest but that we only see them near rivers. Iguanas often use water as an escape route and are good swimmers.

Life Cycle

Iguanas go through several life phases. Starting with the eggs, female iguanas lay them in burrows that they dig themselves. The burrows are usually between 3 and 6 feet (0.9–1.8 m) in length and 12 to 24 inches (30–60 cm) below the surface. They end in a chamber that is large enough to allow the female to turn around. Where populations are dense or where nest sites are scarce, a number of females (sometimes as many as eight) may dig interconnecting tunnels with several entrance holes and egg-laying chambers.

The female green iguana lays a clutch of nine to 71 eggs. In western Costa Rica an average clutch numbers about 35 eggs (it may vary in other localities). Where egg-laying sites are scarce, females may remain near their nests and defend them from other females, which may otherwise dig up the eggs in the course of their own excavations.

The eggs hatch after 65 to 115 days, and clutches often hatch simultaneously. The mass hatching may limit predation, because predators can only eat so many young iguanas at one time. If the eggs hatched over an extended

 SEE ALSO Iguanas **44**:80; Basilisk, Plumed **44**:86

period, the predators would be able to pick off the young lizards as they emerged. Also, large numbers of young iguanas together are more likely to spot potential danger or may even intimidate predators.

Even before they leave their nest chamber, the juveniles eat some soil, which is thought to provide their gut with bacteria that aid digestion. After emerging, they move off into low shrubbery, still maintaining contact with each other. Contact involves tongue licking, rubbing their chins over each other, and nipping each other with their jaws, and is similar to the grooming behavior seen in many social birds and mammals.

The group of young iguanas may forage on the ground at first, but they always sleep on branches, often in small groups. After a few days they move into low shrubs and gradually move farther up into the canopy. By feeding below the adults and larger juveniles, they eat their feces (either deliberately or inadvertently),

⊕ *Green iguanas have small, granular scales and long claws on their fingers and toes to help them climb. The prominent dewlap shows that this individual is a male.*

Tasty Cousin

The genus *Iguana* has one other member, *I. delicatissima*, which means "delicious iguana." Before it became rare, it was valued as food on the Lesser Antilles islands. It is almost identical to the green iguana, but it is slightly smaller and lacks the enlarged scales on its jowls. It was once abundant on every island from Anguilla to Martinique, but habitat destruction, harvesting for food, and introduced predators such as dogs, cats, and mongooses have finished it off on St. Kitts, Nevis, and Antigua. Numbers on the other islands have been reduced to critical levels. To raise awareness of the situation, the Anguilla Post Office issued a set of stamps featuring the species in 1997.

which inoculate their gut with the bacteria needed to help them break down plant material containing cellulose.

Young iguanas have many enemies, including a variety of snakes, birds of prey, and birds such as anis and toucans. A number of small opportunistic mammals, such as coatis and kinkajous, also prey on them. As the iguanas grow, some smaller predators are no longer a problem; but they can attract the attention of larger ones such as crocodiles, caimans, and wild cats. Assuming they survive, they reach breeding size in two or three years. Females and young adult males maintain their green coloration, but they are rarely as bright as the hatchlings. Older males are often gray or tan in color and may turn orange at the height of the breeding season.

Social Behavior and Courtship

A typical colony consists of a large dominant male, a few smaller but also mature males, several subadult males, and four to six females. The large male maintains his dominance by perching at the top of large, prominent rain-forest trees and rarely comes down to the ground. He displays to neighboring males at regular intervals by lowering his large throat flap (dewlap) and nodding his head vigorously.

If close encounters between two large males occur, they raise themselves to their full height, compress their bodies, and lower their dewlaps to make themselves look as large as possible. They circle each other, hissing all the time. If neither is intimidated, they may begin to fight using their long, whiplike tails to thrash each other and bite their opponent's neck until

⬆ *Young green iguanas like this juvenile from Costa Rica are more brightly colored than the adults. Young iguanas mature after about two years; and as they grow, the bright green color fades.*

Spiny-Tailed Iguanas

In Central America the spiny-tailed iguanas, *Ctenosaura* species, are the terrestrial counterparts of the green iguana and are also herbivorous. There are 14 species in the genus altogether, some with small ranges, including the small islands in the Gulf of California, although the most widespread species, *C. similis*, is found from Mexico to Panama. This species is as large as the green iguana but

is less colorful, being pale gray with darker markings. Its tail is strongly banded and has rings of thorny scales around it. Spiny-tailed iguanas dwell among rocks and are often common in forest clearings and around human settlements, where they dig extensive tunnels. Juveniles are bright green and can easily be mistaken for young green iguanas.

⬀ *The clubtail iguana,* Ctenosaura quinquecarinata *from Central America, is a lesser-known relative of the green iguana. Like the other members of its genus, it can be distinguished by the thorny scales around its tail.*

one turns dark and retreats. The dominant male mates with all the females in his territory.

Courtship can last for two weeks or more before the pair finally mate. A male approaches a receptive female from behind and vibrates his head. The female moves her tail to one side, inviting the male to mount her. He continues to bob his head while he climbs on top of her, grips her neck in his jaws, and twists his tail beneath hers so that mating can take place. Small males living nearby look like females, and the large male may not drive them away; in fact, they sometimes try to mate with receptive females while the large male is otherwise occupied.

Once mating is over, females with mature eggs come down from the trees and move to places where they can dig nests. The sites are often open, sandy patches along the riverbank or clearings in the forest. Females may need to travel up to 1.5 miles (2.4 km) to find a suitable egg-laying site.

A significant predator of iguana eggs is the American sunbeam snake, *Loxocemus bicolor*. Although the snake eats a variety of food, including small mammals, frogs, and lizards, it

specializes in digging up reptile nests and eating the eggs. In western Costa Rica where it is fairly common it enters iguana nest tunnels in search of the lizards or digs them out with its pointed snout. First, it slits the iguana eggs to make them collapse, then pushes them against a loop of its body and swallows them whole. One snake that was examined contained 23 green iguana eggs in its stomach, and another had eaten 32 eggs of a spiny-tailed iguana, *Ctenosaura* species.

Large adults are fairly safe from predators (except humans) because of their sheer size. Iguanas basking near water often drop from their branches and swim to safety or disappear under the surface. Females from Barro Colorado Island in Panama even swim to a small, sandy island to lay their eggs.

If they are captured, green iguanas struggle frantically, using their long claws to scratch and tear at their captor and their whiplike tail to thrash it. Handling an angry iguana is no easy matter. Having said that, they are no match for a determined human, and iguanas are routinely sold as food on the streets of Mexico, Guyana, and other parts of Latin America. To reduce the effect on wild populations, iguana "farms" have been set up to provide a supply of animals for both the food and the pet markets.

Coast Horned Lizard

LIZARDS

Phrynosoma coronatum

Horned lizards are among the strangest creatures to inhabit the American Southwest and have always been objects of curiosity among the people of the region.

Common name Coast horned lizard

Scientific name *Phrynosoma coronatum*

Subfamily Phrynosomatinae

Family Iguanidae

Suborder Sauria

Order Squamata

Size From 2.5 in (6 cm) to 4 in (10 cm)

Key features Body flattened and oval or disk shaped; head has a crest, or "coronet," of long, backward-pointing spines, the central 2 (the "horns") being longer than the others; a fringe of smaller thorny spines runs along the edge on each side of its body; large spiny scales also scattered over its back; color yellow, beige, or pale pink with irregular darker crossbands and a paler stripe down the center, providing camouflage colors to match the sand or gravel on which it is resting

Habits Diurnal; terrestrial

Breeding Egg layer with an average of 25 eggs laid in the summer; eggs hatch after about 60 days

Diet Small invertebrates, especially ants

Habitat Dry scrub and sandy washes with scattered bushes; also in dry forest clearings

Distribution Western California south to the tip of Baja California, Mexico

Status Common but easily overlooked

Similar species There are other horned lizards in the American Southwest, but none of their ranges overlap that of this species; the 2 long spines on the back of its head are also distinctive

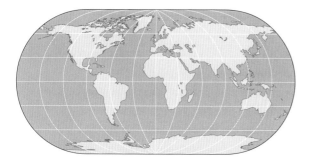

THE ANASAZI INDIANS AND THEIR DESCENDANTS had many stories and superstitions centered on the horned lizard, including beliefs that it could bring about or cure various ailments depending on how it was treated. Stylized horned lizards often feature on pottery, rock paintings, and the small carvings known as fetishes. Modern inhabitants of the Southwest find them no less interesting. They are studied by scientists and kept as pets by well-meaning enthusiasts (usually with poor results). Until recently they were displayed along with rattlesnakes in roadside animal shows, often labeled as "horned toads" (or sometimes "horny toads") because of their squat shape. (The name *Phrynosoma* means "toad bodied.")

Horned lizards are superbly adapted to their environment. In the case of the coast horned lizard the habitat includes the dry woodlands and chaparral as well as desert and semidesert areas in valleys and foothills at elevations up to 6,000 feet (1,830 m).

Early in the morning they often bask with only their head showing above the sand or soil. A mass of capillaries running just under the surface allows their blood to warm up quickly, and from there it moves around the rest of the body. In this way they can reach a temperature at which they can be active without completely exposing themselves and at the same time avoid the possibility of encountering a predator while they are still in a torpid state.

Following this they use their disk-shaped bodies as solar panels, flattening and tilting them toward the sun to absorb as much warmth as possible until they reach their preferred temperature. Only then will they go in

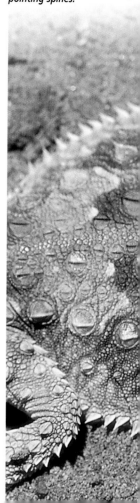

⊕ *The coast horned lizard,* Phrynosoma coronatum, *is relatively large and less rounded than other horned lizards. Its "coronet" is made of long, backward-pointing spines.*

 SEE ALSO Iguanas 44:80; Alligator and Glass Lizards 46:50

⊙ *Like the coast horned lizard, the related P. douglassi, the short-horned lizard, inflates its body to appear bigger and more intimidating when threatened.*

search of food. As the day wears on, they may reorient themselves, contracting their body to a more cylindrical shape and raising themselves off the ground to reduce heat absorption and prevent overheating. At that point other lizards simply seek shade, but horned lizards have an unusual feeding strategy that involves staying out in the open longer than other species.

Ants on the Menu

Horned lizards are ant specialists. Although the proportion of ants in their diet depends on the species, the coast horned lizard is probably typical, with ants making up more than 50 percent of its food. The bones of its skull are modified to make it more effective at snapping up many small food items in rapid succession. Because ants are small and contain a high proportion of indigestible chitin, horned lizards need to eat a lot of them.

They move between anthills until they find a predictable ant trail. Then they sit and wait for the ants to go by, flicking out their tongue and snapping them up one at a time. Only when the supply of ants dries up do they move to another anthill. Their modified skull and large gape may help them flick their tongue in and out rapidly, and they often eat over 200 ants in a single day. To accommodate all the ants, they need a large stomach: Horned lizards' stomachs are proportionately much larger than the stomachs of other lizards of similar overall size. It is the large stomach that gives the horned lizard its short, bulky body plan, and it has other implications too.

Camouflage

Their body shape prevents horned lizards from being swift movers. Although they sometimes scamper into the shelter of a nearby bush, their usual plan is to escape the notice of a predator.

103

They manage to disguise themselves in several ways. First, their coloration always matches the surface on which they live, so coast horned lizards in different parts of the range are different colors depending on the soil type. Because they rely so heavily on camouflage, they tend to remain motionless if they are approached. They crouch low against the ground, where their disklike shape and the fringes of large scales help eliminate shadows and break up their outline—a horned lizard can be nearly impossible to see even when you know where it is!

If the camouflage fails to work, the lizards move on to the next level of defense. They can inflate their body, which has the effect of making them look larger and more intimidating, and also displays their spines more prominently. They tilt their body toward the predator to emphasize their spikiness. Snakes and birds that

clearly did not heed these warnings have been found with horned lizards in their throats and spines sticking out through their skin.

Finally, the last line of defense is to squirt blood. The coast horned lizard is one of several species that can cause small blood vessels around the rim of their eyes to burst, resulting in a thin jet of blood that travels for several inches. Experiments have shown that horned lizards are more likely to squirt blood if they are attacked by members of the dog family (foxes, coyotes, and domestic dogs) than other types of predators. Naturalists have seen the animals drop horned lizards and shake their head vigorously in an effort to get the blood out of their mouth.

Some researchers believe that horned lizards obtain toxins from the ants they eat and store them in their blood to make it taste bitter. If this proves to be the case, the horned lizards would provide an interesting parallel with the poison dart frogs and the mantella frogs (families Mantellidae and Dendrobatidae), which also gather toxins from the bodies of ants they eat and use them for defense.

ⓓ *Phrynosoma cornutum, the Texas horned lizard, is one of several species in the genus that can deter predators by squirting foul-tasting blood from its eyes.*

Large Clutch Sizes

The horned lizard's ant diet is responsible for its rotund body shape and therefore its inability to run quickly. These factors have in turn led to the evolution of cryptic (disguise) coloration and other methods of defense. The carryover effects do not stop there, however. The large body size allows female horned lizards to produce larger clutches of eggs. Not only do they have a greater volume to fill, but the extra bulk of large clutches does not burden the female to the same extent as it would more slender, agile species that rely on speed to escape from predators or to hunt food.

The reproductive effort of reptiles is sometimes measured in terms of relative clutch mass (RCM), which is calculated by dividing the weight of the female by the weight of the eggs or young she produces. Typical RCMs for snakes are about 20 percent; generally speaking, RCMs in lizards are significantly lower. The coast

ⓤ *A newborn short-horned lizard, Phrynosoma hernandesi, in the Chiricahua Mountains of Arizona. Species such as this that live in cool, montane habitats give birth, whereas lowland, desert species are egg layers.*

 SEE ALSO Poison Dart Frogs **43:**68; Mantellas **43:**108; Lizard, Side-Blotched **44:**108; Wall Lizards **45:**58

horned lizard has an RCM approaching 35 percent, which is considerably larger than that of other species from the same region.

The other evolutionary "decision" the coast horned lizard has had to make is whether to direct the reproductive effort into producing a few large eggs or young, or a lot of small ones. In fact, it does the latter. Coast horned lizards have relatively large clutch sizes with an average of 25 and a maximum of 40 eggs. An example of the other extreme is the related side-blotched lizard, *Uta stansburiana*, which lays just one to five eggs.

Eggs or Live Young?

As a rule, species in a single genus either lay eggs or give birth to live young, but there are a few exceptions, including the horned lizards. Of the 13 species six lay eggs and seven are live-bearers. All the live-bearing species live in montane environments that are cooler than the regions inhabited by the egg layers. This is because species that retain their eggs inside their bodies are in a better position to speed up the development of the eggs by basking than those that simply bury them and let the environment provide the heat. On the other hand, species from the warmer lowlands, such as the coast horned lizard, may have time to develop a second clutch before the summer ends (provided they can deposit their first clutch in an early stage of development). In this way they double the potential number of young per year. A very similar situation exists among the alligator lizards in the family Anguidae and the small wall lizards in the family Lacertidae.

Common name Green anole (American chameleon)

Scientific name *Anolis carolinensis*

Subfamily Polychrotinae

Family Iguanidae

Suborder Sauria

Order Squamata

Size From 4.5 in (11 cm) to 8 in (20 cm)

Key features A graceful lizard; head long and narrow; snout pointed; body long and slender; tail is nearly twice as long as head and body combined; legs long and thin; toes have small pads just behind the claws for climbing; color usually bright green but can change to brown or buff; males have a pink dewlap (throat flap)

Habits Diurnal; arboreal, climbing mainly in shrubs and on tree trunks

Breeding Egg layer; female lays several clutches containing a single egg throughout the summer

Diet Small invertebrates

Habitat Open woodland, hedges, parks, and gardens

Distribution Southeastern North America

Status Formerly common, now becoming increasingly rare

Similar species None in the area; small introduced anoles in Florida lack the bright green coloration; the knight anole, *Anolis equestris*, is much larger and lives only in the extreme south of Florida

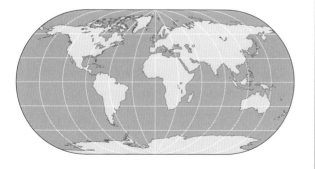

Green Anole

Anolis carolinensis

The green anole is the only member of its genus in the United States, although its relatives have been among the most successful colonizers of Central and South America.

WITH ABOUT 350 SPECIES the genus *Anolis* is one of the most numerous of all lizard genera. Anoles live in South and Central America, especially the West Indies, but the green anole is the only one to occur in the United States, where it is endemic. This colorful lizard was once a familiar sight climbing into low bushes and making graceful leaps in search of prey or flicking its pink dewlap to attract the attention of other members of its species. In recent years its numbers have declined dramatically, perhaps because of competition with introduced species such as the Cuban anole, *Anolis sagrei*, which has done particularly well in its new home.

The green anole is slightly larger than the introduced Cuban species, but it is not as adaptable. Cuban anoles are common wherever they live, setting up territories on and around houses in towns as well as in the countryside. Green anoles also occur in gardens but not to the same extent. The interactions between the two species have not been properly studied, but the fact that one is declining while the other is increasing is a good indicator that competition of one form or another is taking place.

Multiple Clutches

Anoles, unlike the horned lizards, *Phrynosoma* species, are not prolific breeders. Because they rely on speed and agility to catch prey and to evade predators, a bulky clutch of developing eggs would be a real hindrance. To overcome the problem, females mate once and lay several clutches containing a single elongated egg at

① *The green anole can be anything from bright green to brown or gray. Brown phases such as this male from Florida may also be induced when the temperature drops below 70°F (21°C) or if the lizard is threatened or stressed. The usual pink dewlap also turns brown.*

Unsurprisingly, larger and older males are more successful than younger ones at finding mates, but another factor that determines success is activity levels. Males that remain in the same territory defend it easily but only mate with females in that territory. By moving around and continuously setting up new territories, males gain access to more females; but as a result, they come into conflict with other males that may already be present.

regular intervals over a long period. Under ideal conditions females can lay an egg every seven days throughout the spring and summer. Not only does this keep the female's body in good shape, it also allows her to hedge her bets by choosing different egg-laying sites—in a large once-a-year clutch females are gambling with the survival of all their offspring in one go; but by spreading the eggs in different places, there is a better chance of some of them surviving. Eggs are usually laid in damp soil or leaf litter at the base of trees.

Male green anoles are territorial, and their behavior has been studied in greater detail than any of the tropical species. Males display ownership of a territory by rapidly flicking their brightly colored dewlaps up and down. Although the movement can attract predators, when the dewlaps are folded down again, the predator tends to lose sight of the lizard and is left looking for a pink "prey image" rather than a green one.

Species' Recognition

Green anoles in the American Southeast had no need to share their resources with other species until recently when the Cuban anole, *Anolis sagrei*, appeared. Nor could they mistake each other for related anoles and mate with the "wrong" partner. In the Caribbean and elsewhere, however, many species can occur together, and confusion could be a problem. (There are 55 species on Cuba, for example, and 40 on Hispaniola.)

They avoid confusion and direct competition in two ways. First, the various species in a given area occupy different ecological niches. For example, there will be different species living on the ground, in grasses, on bushes, tree trunks, twigs, and in the crowns of forest trees. Second, species' recognition is made easy by having differently colored dewlaps (throat flaps). Within a small area there may be species with orange, yellow, white, or even blue dewlaps, and each responds only to the "correct" color when interacting with others.

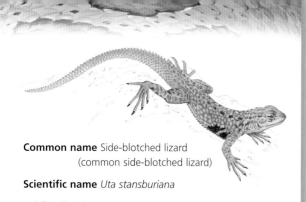

Common name Side-blotched lizard
(common side-blotched lizard)

Scientific name *Uta stansburiana*

Subfamily Phrynosomatinae

Family Iguanidae

Suborder Sauria

Order Squamata

Size From 3 in (7.5 cm) to 5 in (13 cm)

Key features Body small, brownish or gray; small
rounded scales give it a smooth appearance;
no dorsal crest; a dark black or bluish blotch
usually present on either side of the body just
behind the front limbs; males may have blue
flecks and orange or yellow on their throat
and sides

Habits Diurnal; terrestrial, may climb into low shrubs

Breeding Egg layer; female lays several clutches during
the summer; eggs hatch after about 60 days

Diet Insects and other invertebrates

Habitat Anywhere dry; sand dunes and washes,
scrub, places with scattered rocks and thin
woodlands

Distribution Southwestern United States from
Washington to western Texas south to Baja
California, Sonora, and north-central Mexico

Status Very common

Similar species Tree lizard, *Urosaurus microscutatus*, has
a double row of large scales along its midline
interrupted by a single row of small ones
down the center; long-tailed brush lizard,
U. graciosus, has a wide band of large scales
down its back; both lack the characteristic
dark blotch of *Uta stansburiana*

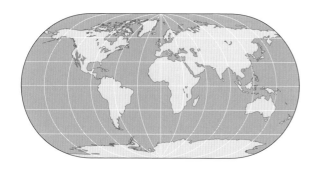

Side-Blotched Lizard

Uta stansburiana

Despite its nondescript appearance, the side-blotched lizard is one of the most important species in the ecology of reptiles in the southwestern United States.

THE SIDE-BLOTCHED LIZARD is one of the most numerous and adaptable species, and it can live in practically any dry environment. It is also one of the most studied lizards anywhere in the world. Because it is so common and can easily be observed during the day, scientists have been able to carry out some interesting research. Much of what they have found out probably applies to several other similar species.

It has a preferred body temperature of 95°F (35°C), substantially lower than that of many other lizards from the region. As a result, it can be active throughout the year in some places, especially in the south of its range. It is an important prey species for many predatory birds and snakes, and in places it may be the main prey of the collared lizards, *Crotaphytus* species.

Sexual Strategies

Careful observations of side-blotched lizard colonies have revealed some interesting sexual behavior. Males fall into one of three categories distinguished by behavior and coloration.

Most mature males have orange throats. They form the first category. They defend large territories that contain a number of females, and they attempt to mate with all of them. Other males have bluish throats. These males do not try to hold down large territories. Instead, they remain with a single female for several days while she is most receptive. In effect, they "guard" the female from other males.

Finally, there are the yellow-throated males. They wander in and out of other males' territories, but they avoid conflict because they look like females. Their strategy is to attempt to mate with females when the territory holder is

SEE ALSO Iguanas **44**:80; Lizard, Collared **44**:88

not looking. They are therefore known as "sneaky" males.

The system is very complicated, but it works well: Sneaky males "steal" matings from territorial males but not from mate-guarding males; territorial males gain almost exclusive access to a number of females but are susceptible to sneaky males; and mate-guarding males protect their females from sneaky males but can be driven off by the more powerful territorial males.

Side-blotched lizards can be very prolific. Females can lay several clutches of up to eight eggs throughout the summer, although there are geographical variations. Winter rainfall seems to be the key to how many eggs they lay: In wetter years the lizards' insect food is more abundant, and they eat enough to divert a large amount of energy into egg production. Gravid females develop orange markings on their flanks to signal to males that they are not receptive to mating.

The side-blotched lizard is very common. Its most distinguishing feature is the blue or black blotch on its side just behind the front legs.

Hatchlings emerge from mid- to late summer. They grow quickly and are sexually mature within a year, so turnover is high. Rapid generation times help species adapt to changing conditions, because the opportunities for variation and mutation are increased.

The Relatives

At some point in the past the side-blotched lizard found its way to several small islands in the Gulf of California, where it evolved into six new species, each with a very small range. Some make a living around seabird colonies, feeding on spilled fish and flies, while others forage for sea slaters along the rocky coastline. They are:

U. palmeri, Palmer's side-blotched lizard from the small island of San Pedro Martír

U. nolascensi from San Pedro Nolascoa, a tiny island between the shores of Baja California and Sonora; unique in the genus because of its bright greenish-blue coloration

U. tumidarostra, the swollen-nosed side-blotched lizard from the island of Coloradito

U. encantadae from the Islas Encantadas

U. squamata from the island of Santa Catalina

U. lowei from the sinister-named Isla El Muerto (Dead-Man Island)

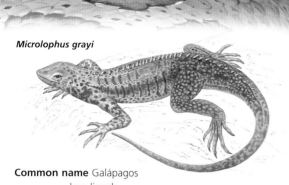

Microlophus grayi

Common name Galápagos
lava lizards

Scientific name *Microlophus* species

Subfamily Tropidurinae

Family Iguanidae

Suborder Sauria

Order Squamata

Number of species 7

Size From 4.8 in (12 cm) to 11.8 in (30 cm); the
Española species, *M. delanonis*, is the largest

Key features Normally proportioned lizards; scales
keeled, giving them a rough appearance;
males have a conspicuous row of large spiny
scales down the middle of their back and
onto their tail; mostly brown with various
light and dark markings according to species;
some have stripes running along their bodies;
females of some species have red throats;
males are larger than females

Habits Terrestrial; diurnal

Breeding Egg layers; females lay clutches of 3–6 eggs
that hatch after about 12 weeks

Diet Mainly insects but also some plant material

Habitat Exposed rocky places where available; also on
sand, including beaches, and among
vegetation

Distribution Galápagos Islands; some species are found
on several islands, while others are endemic
to a single island

Status Common

Similar species None on the islands; the marine and land
iguanas are far bigger, and the only other
lizards are small, nocturnal geckos

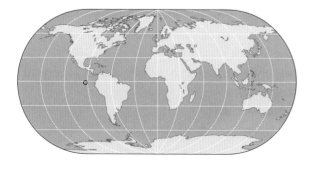

Galápagos Lava Lizards

Microlophus sp.

*Lava lizards are often overshadowed by their larger
and more spectacular relatives, the marine and land
iguanas. However, the varied lava lizards have
interesting stories to tell.*

LAVA LIZARDS ARRIVED ON THE GALÁPAGOS islands
from South America many thousands of years
ago. They spread out and evolved into new
species in the same way as the finches and
tortoises that gave the naturalist Charles Darwin
the inspiration for his theory of natural selection
and the origin of species.

There are seven species of lava lizards
altogether. Islands with plenty of food, such as
Española, have the largest species. On Española
the lava lizards benefit from the seabird colonies
on the island. The birds contribute enormously
to the ecological input of the barren islands by
bringing a constant supply of fish back to their
chicks. Many of the fish are spilled, providing
food for the lizards. In addition, this attracts
flies and other insects, which the lizards also
eat. The seabirds' guano promotes plant
growth, leading in turn to more insects and an
additional food supply for the lizards. It is also
possible that the lizards benefit the seabirds by
eating some of their parasitic ticks and lice.

On the more barren islands with no seabird
colonies, such as San Cristóbal, lava lizards are
smaller and less numerous. Whether this has
always been so or whether their numbers have
fallen since the island's habitats were affected
by introduced goats is impossible to say.

Color Adaptations

Populations of the same species on different
islands or even different parts of the same
island can differ in size and color. The color
differences are due partly to the geology of the
places where they live: Dark lizards live on lava,
while the lighter colored ones live on sand. Lava

 SEE ALSO Iguanas **44**:80; Iguana, Marine **44**:90; Iguana, Galápagos Land **44**:96

lizards on the northern point of Fernandina (such as *M. albemarlensis*, for example) are very small and very dark. They forage around the huge marine iguanas there, often climbing onto their backs in search of small flies to eat.

On Bartolomé, where there are neither marine iguanas nor seabirds in any quantity, the same species is also small but light in color. It feeds on the small white flowers of the mat plant, *Tiquilia nesiotica*. These lizards are nothing if not adaptable!

In some ways, however, they are similar to each other and to their 13 close relatives on the South American mainland from which they originated. Males of all species are highly territorial, usually taking up a stance on top of a boulder or some other prominent lookout place to scout for food, potential mates, and potential rivals. The Fernandina colony will often use a marine iguana's head to stand on

⊕ Male lava lizards are territorial. They will threaten other males by doing "pushups," as seen in this displaying male, Microlophus delanonis from the island of Española.

if there is nothing higher available, and the small posts that mark paths on many islands are also used.

Males display by raising themselves up stiff legged and bobbing slightly: They will even display to human visitors if approached slowly. Many species have deep black "bib" markings on their throats, and some have additional patches of red or orange on their flanks that are visible when the lizard raises itself up. Large males dominate and become tyrants, ferociously chasing off other males, especially during the breeding season.

Bright Females

Unusually among iguanids, females are often more colorful than males. Females of several species have extensive bright reddish-orange patches on the lower half of their head, their throat, and their chest. The reason for the bright coloration is unknown. Females living in rocky places migrate to sandy areas, including the upper reaches of beaches, to dig holes of up to 18 inches (46 cm) deep in which to lay their eggs. They often have to interrupt the digging process from time to time and move into the shade of a bush or rock in order to shelter from the heat.

Typical clutches number three to six eggs, and the females can lay several in the course of a single breeding season. The young hatch after about three months and measure just over 1 inch (3–4 cm) in length. At this stage of their lives they are vulnerable to predation by herons, egrets, mockingbirds, centipedes, and even members of their own species, which are inclined toward cannibalism.

Glossary

Words in SMALL CAPITALS refer to other entries in the glossary.

Acrodont (teeth) teeth attached to the upper edge of the jaw, as opposed to the inside surface (PLEURODONT) or in sockets (THECODONT)

Adaptation a characteristic shape, behavior, or physiological process that equips an organism (or group of related organisms) for its way of life and habitat

Advanced relatively recently evolved (opposite of "primitive")

Albino an animal that has no color pigment in its body and has red eyes

Amniotic egg an egg with a fluid-filled sac within a membrane that encloses the embryo of reptiles, birds, and mammals. Animals that produce amniotic eggs are known as amniotes

Amplexus the position adopted during mating in most frogs and many salamanders, in which the male clasps the female with one or both pairs of limbs. See AXILLARY AMPLEXUS and INGUINAL AMPLEXUS

Annuli the growth rings often visible on the shell of CHELONIANS

Anterior the front part or head and shoulders of an animal

Aposematic coloration bright coloration serving to warn a potential predator that an animal is distasteful or poisonous

Arboreal living in trees or shrubs

Autotomy self-amputation of part of the body. Some lizards practice CAUDAL autotomy: They discard all or part of their tail

Axillary amplexus mating position in frogs in which the male grasps the female behind her front limbs. See INGUINAL AMPLEXUS

Barbel a small, elongated "feeler," or sensory process, on the head, usually of aquatic animals, e.g., some pipid frogs

Binocular vision the ability to focus both eyes on a single subject. The eyes must point forward (not sideways as in most reptiles and amphibians). Binocular vision enables animals, including humans, to judge distances

Bridges the sides of a turtle's shell, attaching to the CARAPACE above and the PLASTRON below

Brille the transparent covering over the eyes of snakes and some lizards, such as geckos

Bromeliad member of a family of plants restricted to the New World. Many live attached to trees, including "urn plants" in which ARBOREAL frogs sometimes breed

Calcareous containing calcium carbonate

Carapace the upper part of the shell of turtles and tortoises, the other parts being the PLASTRON and the BRIDGES. Also used to describe the hard structure covering part of any animal's body

Caudal relating to the tail, as in subcaudal scales beneath a snake's tail and caudal (tail) fin

Chelonian a member of the ORDER Chelonia, containing all reptiles variously known as terrapins, turtles, and tortoises

Chromatophore a specialized cell containing pigment, usually located in the outer layers of the skin

Chromosome a thread-shaped structure consisting largely of genetic material (DNA), found in the nucleus of cells

Cirrus (pl. cirri) a slender, usually flexible appendage on an animal

CITES an international conservation organization: Convention on International Trade in Endangered Species

Class a TAXONOMIC category ranking below PHYLUM, containing a number of ORDERS

Cloaca the common chamber into which the urinary, digestive, and reproductive systems discharge their contents, and which opens to the exterior; from Latin meaning "sewer" or "drain"

Clutch the eggs laid by a female at one time

Continuous breeder an animal that may breed at any time of year

Convergent evolution the effect of unrelated animals looking like each other because they have adapted to similar conditions in similar ways

Coprophagy the practice of eating excrement

Costal relating to the ribs

Costal grooves grooves or folds along the flanks of caecilians and some salamanders that correspond to the position of the ribs

Crocodilian a member of the order Crocodylia, including alligators, caimans, crocodiles, and gharials

Cryptic having the ability to remain hidden, usually by means of camouflage, e.g., cryptic coloration

Cutaneous respiration breathing that takes place across the skin's surface, especially important in amphibians

Cycloid disklike, resembling a circle

Denticle toothlike scale

Dermis layer of skin immediately below the EPIDERMIS

Dewlap flap or fold of skin under an animal's throat. Sometimes used in displays, e.g., in anole lizards

Dimorphism the existence of two distinct forms within a SPECIES, which is then said to be dimorphic. In species in which there are more than two forms, they are polymorphic. See SEXUAL DIMORPHISM

Direct development transition from egg to the adult form in amphibians without passing through a free-living LARVAL stage

Dorsal relating to the back or upper surface of the body or one of its parts

Ectotherm (adj. ectothermic) an animal that relies on external heat sources, such as the sun, to raise its body temperature. Reptiles and amphibians are ectotherms. See ENDOTHERM

Eft juvenile, TERRESTRIAL phase in the life cycle of a newt. The red eft is the terrestrial juvenile form of the eastern newt, *Notophthalmus viridescens*

Egg tooth small toothlike scale that some amphibians and reptiles have on the tip of the snout to assist in breaking through their eggshell

Endemic SPECIES, GENERA, OR FAMILIES that are restricted to a particular geographical region

Endotherm (adj. endothermic) an animal that can sustain a high body temperature by means of heat generated within the body by the metabolism. See ECTOTHERM

Epidermis surface layer of the skin of a vertebrate

Epiphyte plant growing on another plant but not a parasite. Includes many orchids and BROMELIADS and some mosses and ferns

Estivation a state of inactivity during prolonged periods of drought or high temperature. During estivation the animal often buries itself in soil or mud. See HIBERNATION

Estuarine living in the lower part of a river (estuary) where fresh water meets and mixes with seawater

Explosive breeder a SPECIES in which the breeding season is very short, resulting in large numbers of animals mating at the same time

External fertilization fusing of eggs and sperm outside the female's body, as in nearly all frogs and toads. See INTERNAL FERTILIZATION

Family TAXONOMIC category ranking below ORDER, containing GENERA that are more closely related to one another than any other grouping of genera

Farming hatching and rearing of young CHELONIANS and CROCODILIANS from a captive-breeding population. See RANCHING

Fauna the animal life of a locality or region

Femoral gland gland situated on an animal's thigh

Femoral pores row of pores along an animal's thighs. Most obvious in many lizards

Fertilization union of an egg and a sperm

Gamete OVUM or sperm

Genus (pl. genera) taxonomic category ranking below FAMILY; a group of SPECIES all more closely related to one another than to any other group of species

Gestation carrying the developing young within the body. Gestation period is the length of time that this occurs

Gill respiratory structure in aquatic animals through which gas exchange takes place

Gill slits slits in which GILLS are situated and present in some amphibians and their LARVAE

Granular (scale) small grainlike scales covering the body, as in some geckos and in the file snakes, *Acrochordus*

Gravid carrying eggs or young

Gular pouch area of expandable skin in the throat region

Hedonic glands glands in a male salamander that stimulate a female when they are rubbed against her body

Heliotherm an animal that basks to regulate body temperature

Hemipenis (pl. hemipenes) one of two grooved copulatory structures present in the males of some reptiles

Herbivore animal that eats plants

Heterogeneous (scales) scales that differ in shape or size. See HOMOGENEOUS (SCALES)

Hibernation a period of inactivity, often spent underground, to avoid extremes of cold. See ESTIVATION

Hinge a means by which the PLASTRON of some CHELONIANS can be pulled up, giving the reptile more protection against a would-be predator

Home range an area in which an animal lives except for MIGRATIONS or rare excursions

Homogeneous (scales) scales that are all the same shape and size. See HETEROGENEOUS (SCALES)

Hyoid "u"-shaped bone at the base of the tongue to which the larynx is attached

Inguinal pertaining to the groin

Inguinal amplexus a mating position in which a male frog or salamander clasps a female around the lower abdomen. See AXILLARY AMPLEXUS

Intergular scute a single plate, or SCUTE, lying between the paired gular scutes on the PLASTRON of side-necked turtles

Internal fertilization fusing of eggs and sperm inside the female's body, as in reptiles and most salamanders. See EXTERNAL FERTILIZATION

Interstitial the thin skin between the scales of reptiles. Sometimes called "interscalar" skin

Introduced species brought from lands where it occurs naturally to lands where it has not previously occurred

IUCN International Union for the Conservation of Nature, responsible for assigning animals and plants to internationally agreed categories of rarity. *See* table below

Jacobson's organ (or vomeronasal organ) one of a pair of grooves extending from the nasal cavity and opening into the mouth cavity in some mammals and reptiles. Molecules collected on the tongue are sampled by this organ, which supplements the sense of smell

Juvenile young animal, not sexually mature

Karst a porous form of limestone

Keeled scales a ridge on the DORSAL scales of some snakes

Keratophagy the practice of eating molted skin

Lamella (pl. lamellae) thin transverse plates across the undersides of the toes of some lizards, especially geckos

Larva (pl. larvae) early stage in the development of an animal (including amphibians) after hatching from the egg

Lateral line organ sense organ embedded in the skin of some aquatic animals, including LARVAL salamanders and some frogs, which responds to waterborne vibrations. Usually arranged in a row along the animal's side

Leucistic an animal that lacks all pigment except that in its eyes. Partially leucistic animals have patches of white over an otherwise normally pigmented skin. See ALBINO

Life cycle complete life history of an organism from one stage to the recurrence of that stage, e.g., egg to egg

Life history history of a single individual organism from the fertilization of the egg until its death

Lifestyle general mode of life of an animal, e.g., NOCTURNAL predator, aquatic HERBIVORE, parasite

Live-bearing giving birth to young that have developed beyond the egg stage. Live-bearers may be VIVIPAROUS or OVOVIVIPAROUS

Lure (noun) part of the body, such as the tail, that is used to entice prey closer

Mental gland gland on the chin of some newts and salamanders that appears to stimulate the female during courtship; one of the HEDONIC GLANDS

Metabolism chemical or energy changes occurring within a living organism that are involved in various life activities

Metamorphosis transformation of an animal from one stage of its life history to another, e.g., from LARVA to adult

Microenvironment local conditions that immediately surround an organism

Migration movement of animals from one place to another, often in large numbers and often for breeding purposes

Mimic an animal that resembles an animal belonging to another SPECIES, usually a distasteful or venomous one, or some inedible object

Milt sperm-containing fluid produced by a male frog during egg laying to fertilize the eggs

Montane pertaining to mountains or SPECIES that live in mountains

Morph form or phase of an animal

Morphological relating to the form and structure of an organism

Nasolabial groove a groove running from the nostril to the upper lip in male plethodontid salamanders

Neonate the newborn young of a live-bearer

Neoteny condition in which a LARVA fails to METAMORPHOSE and retains its larval features as an adult. Species with this condition are said to be neotenic. The axolotl is the best-known example. See PEDOMORPHOSIS

Neotropics the tropical part of the New World, including northern South America, Central America, part of Mexico, and the West Indies

Newt amphibious salamanders of the genera *Triturus, Taricha,* and *Notophthalmus*

Niche the role played by a SPECIES in its particular community. It is determined by its food and temperature preferences; each species' niche within a community is unique

Nocturnal active at night

Nuptial pad an area of dark, rough skin that develops in male amphibians on the hands, arms, or chest of some SPECIES prior to the breeding season. Its purpose is to allow the male to grip the female in AMPLEXUS

Occipital lobe the pyramid-shaped area at the back of the brain that helps an animal interpret vision

Ocular of the eye

Olfactory relating to the sense of smell

Omnivore an animal that eats both animal and plant material

Order taxonomic category ranking below CLASS and above FAMILY

Osteoderm small bone in the skin of some reptiles; lies under the scales

Ovary female gonad or reproductive organ that produces the OVUM

Overwinter survive the winter

Oviduct the duct in females that carries the OVUM from the ovary to the CLOACA

Oviparous reproducing by eggs that hatch outside the female's body

IUCN CATEGORIES

EX **Extinct,** when there is no reasonable doubt that the last individual of the species has died.

EW **Extinct in the Wild,** when a species is known only to survive in captivity or as a naturalized population well outside the past range.

CR **Critically Endangered,** when a species is facing an extremely high risk of extinction in the wild in the immediate future.

EN **Endangered,** when a species is facing a very high risk of extinction in the wild in the near future.

VU **Vulnerable,** when a species is facing a high risk of extinction in the wild in the medium-term future.

LR **Lower Risk,** when a species has been evaluated and does not satisfy the criteria for CR, EN, or VU.

DD **Data Deficient,** when there is not enough information about a species to assess the risk of extinction.

NE **Not Evaluated,** species that have not been assessed by the IUCN criteria.

Ovoviviparous reproducing by eggs that the female retains within her body until they hatch; the developing eggs contain a yolk sac but receive no nourishment from the mother through a placenta or similar structure

Ovum (pl. ova) female germ cell or GAMETE; an egg cell or egg

Papilla (pl. papillae) aised projection(s) of soft tissue often seen on the head and neck of aquatic CHELONIANS

Parietal eye a VESTIGIAL eye situated in the top of the head of tuataras and some lizards, sometimes known as the "third eye"

Parietals pairs of bones forming the rear of the roof of the brain case

Parotid glands pair of large glands on the shoulder, neck, or behind the eye in some salamanders and toads

Parthenogenesis a form of asexual reproduction in which the OVUM develops without being fertilized. Such SPECIES are said to be parthenogenetic

Parturition the process of giving birth to live young

Pectoral girdle the skeleton supporting the forelimbs of a land vertebrate

Pedogenesis form of reproduction by an animal still showing LARVAL characteristics

Pedomorphosis the retention of immature or LARVAL characteristics, such as GILLS, by animals that are sexually mature. See NEOTENY

Permeable property of a substance, such as skin, allowing another substance, such as water, to pass through it

Pheromone a substance released by an organism to induce a response in another individual of the same SPECIES, such as sexual attraction

Phylum taxonomic category ranking above CLASS and below kingdom

Pigment a substance that gives color to part or all of an organism's body

Plastron the ventral portion, or underside, of the shell of a turtle

Pleurodont teeth teeth that are attached to the inside surface of the jaw, as opposed to the upper edge (ACRODONT) or in sockets (THECODONT)

Pond-type larva salamander LARVA with high fins and a deep body, adapted to living in still water. See STREAM-TYPE LARVA

Preanal pores chemical- or pheromone-secreting pores in front of the CLOACA, usually in lizards

Prehensile adapted for grasping or clasping, especially by wrapping around, such as the tail of chameleons

Preocular relating to the front of the eye

Ranching artificial incubation of eggs collected from the wild followed by captive-rearing of the young. A method used with both CHELONIANS and CROCODILIANS to increase population numbers, carried out in an environment free from predators

Rectilinear locomotion a form of movement used by heavy-bodied snakes in which the body progresses in a straight line

Riffle agitated water flowing over rocks or gravel in shallow streams or rivers

Rostral processes extensions to the snout, including horns and other ornamentation

Salt glands glands located in the vicinity of the eye that allow marine turtles and some CROCODILIANS to excrete excessive salt from their bodies, helping prevent them from becoming dehydrated in the marine environment

Satellite male a male frog that does not call but sits near a calling male and intercepts females attracted to the calling male

Savanna open grasslands with scattered trees and bushes, usually in warm areas

Scute enlarged scale on a reptile, including the colorful scales that cover the shell of turtles; divided into different groups, such as the vertebral scutes that run above the VERTEBRAL COLUMN

Sexual dimorphism the existence of marked morphological differences between males and females

Species taxonomic category ranking below GENUS; a group of organisms with common attributes capable of interbreeding and producing healthy fertile offspring

Spermatheca a pouch or sac in the female reproductive tract in which sperm are stored

Spermatophore a structure containing sperm that is passed from the male to the female in some animals, such as in many salamanders

Stream-type larva streamlined LARVA with low fins and elongated body, adapted for living in flowing water. See POND-TYPE LARVA

Subcaudal beneath the tail, as in "subcaudal" scales. See CAUDAL

Subocular usually refers to scales below the eye. See PREOCULAR

Subspecies a locally distinct group of animals that differ slightly from the normal appearance of the SPECIES; often called a race

Substrate the solid material on which an organism lives, e.g., sand, mud, etc.

Suture the zigzag patterning formed beneath the SCUTES where the bones of a CHELONIAN's shell fuse together

Tadpole LARVAL stage of a frog or toad

Talus slopes slopes covered with loose rocks and slabs. Also known as scree

Taxonomy the science of classification: the arrangement of animals and plants into groups based on their natural relationships

Temporal relating to the area between the eye and ear

Terrestrial living on land

Territorial defending an area so as to exclude other members of the same SPECIES

Territory an area that one or more animals defends against other members of the same SPECIES

Thecodont teeth growing in sockets. See ACRODONT

Thermoregulate to expose to or move away from a heat source in order to maintain desired body temperature

Thermoregulation control of body temperature by behavioral or physiological means, so that it maintains a constant or near-constant value

Thyroid gland a gland lying in the neck that produces the hormone THYROXINE

Thyroxine a hormone containing iodine that is involved in a variety of physiological processes, including METAMORPHOSIS in amphibians

Toad any stout-bodied, warty-skinned frog, especially one living away from water. The term has no TAXONOMIC basis, although members of the FAMILY Bufonidae are often called toads

Tongue-flicking constant use of the tongue by snakes and some lizards when exploring their surroundings. Used in conjunction with JACOBSON'S ORGAN

Tubercle a small, knoblike projection

Turtle any shelled reptile, including tortoises and terrapins

Tympanum (pl. tympana) eardrum

Unisexual species a SPECIES consisting only of females, in which reproduction is by PARTHENOGENESIS

Unken reflex a defensive posture shown by some amphibians when attacked, in which the body is arched inward with the head and tail lifted upward. Its purpose is to display a brightly colored underside

Uterine milk a uterine secretion that provides developing embryos with nourishment

Vent the CLOACAL opening of the body. Measurements of reptiles and amphibians are often given as "snout-vent" lengths or simply "s-v" lengths

Ventral describing the lower surface of the body or one of its parts

Vertebral column the spinal skeleton, or backbone, consisting of a series of vertebrae extending from the skull to the tip of the tail

Vertebrate a member of the subphylum Vertebrata, comprising all animals with a VERTEBRAL COLUMN, including fish, amphibians, reptiles, birds, and mammals

Vestigial smaller and of more simple structure than in an evolutionary ancestor. In reptiles and amphibians often used to describe limbs that have become reduced in size through the evolutionary process

Viviparous giving birth to living young that develop within and are nourished by the mother. Often used incorrectly, however, to describe any live-bearing species. See also OVOVIVIPAROUS

Volar pores pores on the underside of the feet

Webbing folds of skin present between the toes of both CROCODILIANS and aquatic CHELONIANS

Xeric adapted to life in an extremely dry habitat

Yolk sac a large sac containing stored nutrients, present in the embryos of fish, amphibians, reptiles, and birds

Further Reading

General

Arnold, E. N., *A Field Guide to the Reptiles and Amphibians of Britain and Europe*, Harper Collins, London, 2002

Behler, J. L., and King, F. W., *The Audubon Society Field Guide to North American Reptiles and Amphibians*, Alfred A. Knopf, New York, 1979

Branch, W. R., *Field Guide to the Snakes and Other Reptiles of Southern Africa*, Struik, Cape Town, 1998

Cloudsley-Thompson, J. L., *The Temperature and Water Relations of Reptiles*, Merrow, London, 1971

Cogger, H. G., *Reptiles and Amphibians of Australia*, 6th edn., Reed New Holland, Sydney, 2000

Glaw, F., and Vences, M., *A Field Guide to the Reptiles and Amphibians of Madagascar*, 2nd edn., published by the authors, Bonn, 1994

Grismer, L. L., *Amphibians and Reptiles of Baja California*, University of California Press, Berkeley, CA, 2002

Halliday, T., and Adler, C. (eds.), *The New Encyclopedia of Reptiles and Amphibians*, Firefly Books, New York and Toronto/Oxford University Press, Oxford, 2002

Murphy, J. B., Adler, K., and Collins, J. T. (eds.), *Captive Management and Conservation of Reptiles and Amphibians*, Society for the Study of Amphibians and Reptiles, Ithaca, NY, 1994

Savage, J. M., *Amphibians and Reptiles of Costa Rica*, University of Chicago Press, Chicago, 2002

Schleich, H. H., Kästle, W., and Kabisch, K., *Amphibians and Reptiles of North Africa*, Koeltz Scientific Books, Koenigstien, 1996

Spawls, S., Howell, K., Drewes, R., and Ashe, J., *A Field Guide to the Reptiles of East Africa*, Academic Press, London, 2002

Zug, G. R., Vitt, L. J., and Caldwell, J. P., *Herpetology: An Introductory Biology of Reptiles and Amphibians*, 2nd edn., Academic Press, San Diego, 2001

Specific to this volume

Anderson, S. C., *The Lizards of Iran*, Society for the Study of Amphibians and Reptiles, Ithaca, NY, 1999

Martin, J., *Chameleons: Nature's Masters of Disguise*, Facts on File, New York, 1992

Pianka, E. R., *Ecology and Natural History of Desert Lizards*, Princeton University Press, Princeton, NJ, 1986

Pianka, E. R., and Vitt, L. J., *Lizards: Windows to the Evolution of Diversity*, University of California Press, Berkeley, CA, 2003

Sherbrooke, W. C., *Introduction to Horned Lizards of North America*, University of California Press, Berkeley, CA, 2003

Smith, H. M., *Handbook of Lizards*, Cornell University Press, Ithaca, NY, 1995

Storr, G. M., Smith, L. A., and Johnstone, R. E., *Lizards of Western Australia*, parts 1, 2, and 3, Western Australian Museum, Perth, 1981, 1983, 1990

Useful Websites

General

Myers, P. 2001. "Vertebrata" (On-line), Animal Diversity. Accessible at: **http://animaldiversity.ummz.umich.edu/site/accounts/information/Reptilia.html**

http://www.embl-heidelberg.de/~uetz/LivingReptiles.html
The University of Heidelberg reptile database. List of species with bibliographies and links to important references

http://www.herplit.com/
A listing of herpetological literature, including older material

http://www.kingsnake.com
Many pages about reptiles and amphibians, especially their care in captivity, and links to other organizations

http://www.redlist.org
IUCN Red List gives details of all threatened animals, including reptiles and amphibians

http://www.si.edu/resource/faq/nmnh/zoology.htm#vz
General information about reptiles and amphibians and links to many educational sites

http://tolweb.org/tree/
A collaborative Internet project produced by biologists from around the world, containing information about the diversity of organisms on earth, their history, and characteristics

Specific to this volume

http://www.greenigsociety.org/
Website of the Green Iguana Society provides information on iguana care as well as details of current iguana adoption and rescues throughout the United States and Canada

http://www.nafcon.dircon.co.uk/agamids.html
Provides detailed information about agamids

http://www.repticzone.com/
A website providing information on reptiles and amphibians. Includes useful links to caresheets for agamas, chameleons, and iguanas

Set Index

A **bold** number shows the volume and is followed by the relevant page numbers (e.g., **21:** 52, 74).

Common names in **bold** (e.g., **adder**) mean that the animal has an illustrated main entry in the set. Underlined page numbers (e.g., **29:** 78–79) refer to the main entry for that animal.

Italic page numbers (e.g., **22:** 103) point to illustrations of animals in parts of the set other than the main entry.

Page numbers in parentheses—e.g., **21:** (24)—locate information in At-a-Glance boxes.

Animals that have main entries in the set are indexed under their common names, alternative common names, and scientific names.

Picture Credits

Abbreviations

A Ardea, London; BCL Bruce Coleman Limited; CM Chris Mattison; FLPA Frank Lane Picture Agency; NHPA Natural History Photographic Agency; NPL Naturepl.com; PW Premaphotos Wildlife; P.com/OSF Photolibrary.com/Oxford Scientific Films; SPL Science Photo Library

t = top; **b** = bottom; **c** = center; **l** = left; **r** = right

Jacket: tl Geoff Trinder/A; **tr** Martin Harvey/NHPA; **bl** John Cancalosi/A; **br** Marty Cordano/P.com/OSF

9 Mike Brown/P.com/OSF; **14** CM; **14–15** Adrian Warren/A; **16** Pete Oxford/NPL; **19** Kevin Schafer/Corbis; **20–21** Heather Angel/Natural Visions; **23** Robin Bush/P.com/OSF; **24–25** Masahiro Iijima/A; **25** Minden Pictures/FLPA; **26t, 26b** CM; **27** David Welling/NPL; **28** Michael Fogden/P.com/OSF; **29** Walter Rohdich/FLPA; **30** CM; **31** Claudio Velasquez/NPL; **33t** CM; **33b** Winifred Wisniewski/FLPA; **34–35** Daniel Heuclin/NHPA; **36** Mirko Stelzner/NHPA; **37** J.W.W. Louwman/FLPA; **38–39** Daniel Heuclin/NHPA; **39** CM; **40–41** Wendy Dennis/FLPA; **43** Dave Watts/NHPA; **45** Stephen Dalton/NHPA; **47** Elio Della Ferrera/NPL; **49** Steven D. Miller/NPL; **51** William Osborn/NPL; **53t** Brian Kenney/P.com/OSF; **53b** Daniel Heuclin/NHPA; **54t** CM; **54–55** Heather Angel/Natural Visions; **57** CM; **58t** Zig Leszczynski, AA/P.com/OSF; **58b** CM; **60b, 60–61** Pete Oxford/NPL; **63** Wendy Dennis/FLPA; **65** Pete Oxford/NPL; **67** Heather Angel/Natural Visions; **69** Alberto Nardi/NHPA; **71** Stephen Dalton/NHPA; **73** Ingo Arndt/NPL; **75** CM; **76l** Tom Ulrich/P.com/OSF; **76r** Nick Garbutt/NPL; **77** Marian Bacon, AA/P.com/OSF; **79** CM; **83** James Carmichael jr./NHPA; **84–85** Richard Day/Natural Visions; **85** Zig Leszczynski, AA/P.com/OSF; **87** James Carmichael jr/NHPA; **89** Brian Kenney/P.com/OSF; **90–91** T.D. Roy, Minden Pictures/FLPA; **91** Tony Heald/NPL; **92** D.Parer & E. Parer-Cook/A; **93** CM; **94–95** D.Parer & E. Parer-Cook/A; **97** David Hosking/FLPA; **99** John Daniels/A; **100** Doug Wechsler/NPL; Brian Kenney/P.com/OSF; **102–103** CM; **103** Marty Cordano/P.com/OSF; **104** Raymond Mendez, AA/P.com/OSF; **105** CM; **107** Steven D. Miller/NPL; **109** Zig Leszczynski, AA/P.com/OSF; **111** CM